FREE Study Skills Videos/DVD Offer

Dear Customer,

Thank you for your purchase from Mometrix! We consider it an honor and a privilege that you have purchased our product and we want to ensure your satisfaction.

As part of our ongoing effort to meet the needs of test takers, we have developed a set of Study Skills Videos that we would like to give you for <u>FREE</u>. These videos cover our *best practices* for getting ready for your exam, from how to use our study materials to how to best prepare for the day of the test.

All that we ask is that you email us with feedback that would describe your experience so far with our product. Good, bad, or indifferent, we want to know what you think!

To get your FREE Study Skills Videos, you can use the **QR code** below, or send us an **email** at <u>studyvideos@mometrix.com</u> with *FREE VIDEOS* in the subject line and the following information in the body of the email:

- The name of the product you purchased.
- Your product rating on a scale of 1-5, with 5 being the highest rating.
- Your feedback. It can be long, short, or anything in between. We just want to know your impressions and experience so far with our product. (Good feedback might include how our study material met your needs and ways we might be able to make it even better. You could highlight features that you found helpful or features that you think we should add.)

If you have any questions or concerns, please don't hesitate to contact me directly.

Thanks again!

Sincerely,

Jay Willis
Vice President
<u>jay.willis@mometrix.com</u>
1-800-673-8175

GMAT

Prep Book 2025-2026

GMAT Exam Secrets Study Guide

Full-Length Practice Test

Step-by-Step Video Tutorials

8th Edition

Written and edited by Matthew Bowling

Printed in the United States of America

This paper meets the requirements of ANSI/NISO Z39.48-1992 (Permanence of Paper).

Mometrix offers volume discount pricing to institutions. For more information or a price quote, please contact our sales department at sales@mometrix.com or 888-248-1219.

Mometrix Media LLC is not affiliated with or endorsed by any official testing organization. All organizational and test names are trademarks of their respective owners.

ISBN 13: 978-1-5167-2746-9
ISBN 10: 1-5167-2746-0

DEAR FUTURE EXAM SUCCESS STORY

First of all, **THANK YOU** for purchasing Mometrix study materials!

Second, congratulations! You are one of the few determined test-takers who are committed to doing whatever it takes to excel on your exam. **You have come to the right place.** We developed these study materials with one goal in mind: to deliver you the information you need in a format that's concise and easy to use.

In addition to optimizing your guide for the content of the test, we've outlined our recommended steps for breaking down the preparation process into small, attainable goals so you can make sure you stay on track.

We've also analyzed the entire test-taking process, identifying the most common pitfalls and showing how you can overcome them and be ready for any curveball the test throws you.

Standardized testing is one of the biggest obstacles on your road to success, which only increases the importance of doing well in the high-pressure, high-stakes environment of test day. Your results on this test could have a significant impact on your future, and this guide provides the information and practical advice to help you achieve your full potential on test day.

Your success is our success

We would love to hear from you! If you would like to share the story of your exam success or if you have any questions or comments in regard to our products, please contact us at **800-673-8175** or **support@mometrix.com**.

Thanks again for your business and we wish you continued success!

Sincerely,
The Mometrix Test Preparation Team

> **Need more help? Check out our flashcards at:**
> **http://MometrixFlashcards.com/GMAT**

TABLE OF CONTENTS

Introduction

Thank you for purchasing this resource! You have made the choice to prepare yourself for a test that could have a huge impact on your future, and this guide is designed to help you be fully ready for test day. Obviously, it's important to have a solid understanding of the test material, but you also need to be prepared for the unique environment and stressors of the test, so that you can perform to the best of your abilities.

For this purpose, the first section that appears in this guide is the **Secret Keys**. We've devoted countless hours to meticulously researching what works and what doesn't, and we've boiled down our findings to the five most impactful steps you can take to improve your performance on the test. We start at the beginning with study planning and move through the preparation process, all the way to the testing strategies that will help you get the most out of what you know when you're finally sitting in front of the test.

We recommend that you start preparing for your test as far in advance as possible. However, if you've bought this guide as a last-minute study resource and only have a few days before your test, we recommend that you skip over the first two Secret Keys since they address a long-term study plan.

If you struggle with **test anxiety**, we strongly encourage you to check out our recommendations for how you can overcome it. Test anxiety is a formidable foe, but it can be beaten, and we want to make sure you have the tools you need to defeat it.

Secret Key #1 – Plan Big, Study Small

There's a lot riding on your performance. If you want to ace this test, you're going to need to keep your skills sharp and the material fresh in your mind. You need a plan that lets you review everything you need to know while still fitting in your schedule. We'll break this strategy down into three categories.

Information Organization

Start with the information you already have: the official test outline. From this, you can make a complete list of all the concepts you need to cover before the test. Organize these concepts into groups that can be studied together, and create a list of any related vocabulary you need to learn so you can brush up on any difficult terms. You'll want to keep this vocabulary list handy once you actually start studying since you may need to add to it along the way.

Time Management

Once you have your set of study concepts, decide how to spread them out over the time you have left before the test. Break your study plan into small, clear goals so you have a manageable task for each day and know exactly what you're doing. Then just focus on one small step at a time. When you manage your time this way, you don't need to spend hours at a time studying. Studying a small block of content for a short period each day helps you retain information better and avoid stressing over how much you have left to do. You can relax knowing that you have a plan to cover everything in time. In order for this strategy to be effective though, you have to start studying early and stick to your schedule. Avoid the exhaustion and futility that comes from last-minute cramming!

Study Environment

The environment you study in has a big impact on your learning. Studying in a coffee shop, while probably more enjoyable, is not likely to be as fruitful as studying in a quiet room. It's important to keep distractions to a minimum. You're only planning to study for a short block of time, so make the most of it. Don't pause to check your phone or get up to find a snack. It's also important to **avoid multitasking**. Research has consistently shown that multitasking will make your studying dramatically less effective. Your study area should also be comfortable and well-lit so you don't have the distraction of straining your eyes or sitting on an uncomfortable chair.

 The time of day you study is also important. You want to be rested and alert. Don't wait until just before bedtime. Study when you'll be most likely to comprehend and remember. Even better, if you know what time of day your test will be, set that time aside for study. That way your brain will be used to working on that subject at that specific time and you'll have a better chance of recalling information.

Finally, it can be helpful to team up with others who are studying for the same test. Your actual studying should be done in as isolated an environment as possible, but the work of organizing the information and setting up the study plan can be divided up. In between study sessions, you can discuss with your teammates the concepts that you're all studying and quiz each other on the details. Just be sure that your teammates are as serious about the test as you are. If you find that your study time is being replaced with social time, you might need to find a new team.

Secret Key #2 – Make Your Studying Count

You're devoting a lot of time and effort to preparing for this test, so you want to be absolutely certain it will pay off. This means doing more than just reading the content and hoping you can remember it on test day. It's important to make every minute of study count. There are two main areas you can focus on to make your studying count.

Retention

It doesn't matter how much time you study if you can't remember the material. You need to make sure you are retaining the concepts. To check your retention of the information you're learning, try recalling it at later times with minimal prompting. Try carrying around flashcards and glance at one or two from time to time or ask a friend who's also studying for the test to quiz you.

To enhance your retention, look for ways to put the information into practice so that you can apply it rather than simply recalling it. If you're using the information in practical ways, it will be much easier to remember. Similarly, it helps to solidify a concept in your mind if you're not only reading it to yourself but also explaining it to someone else. Ask a friend to let you teach them about a concept you're a little shaky on (or speak aloud to an imaginary audience if necessary). As you try to summarize, define, give examples, and answer your friend's questions, you'll understand the concepts better and they will stay with you longer. Finally, step back for a big picture view and ask yourself how each piece of information fits with the whole subject. When you link the different concepts together and see them working together as a whole, it's easier to remember the individual components.

Finally, practice showing your work on any multi-step problems, even if you're just studying. Writing out each step you take to solve a problem will help solidify the process in your mind, and you'll be more likely to remember it during the test.

Modality

Modality simply refers to the means or method by which you study. Choosing a study modality that fits your own individual learning style is crucial. No two people learn best in exactly the same way, so it's important to know your strengths and use them to your advantage.

For example, if you learn best by visualization, focus on visualizing a concept in your mind and draw an image or a diagram. Try color-coding your notes, illustrating them, or creating symbols that will trigger your mind to recall a learned concept. If you learn best by hearing or discussing information, find a study partner who learns the same way or read aloud to yourself. Think about how to put the information in your own words. Imagine that you are giving a lecture on the topic and record yourself so you can listen to it later.

For any learning style, flashcards can be helpful. Organize the information so you can take advantage of spare moments to review. Underline key words or phrases. Use different colors for different categories. Mnemonic devices (such as creating a short list in which every item starts with the same letter) can also help with retention. Find what works best for you and use it to store the information in your mind most effectively and easily.

3

Secret Key #3 – Practice the Right Way

Your success on test day depends not only on how many hours you put into preparing, but also on whether you prepared the right way. It's good to check along the way to see if your studying is paying off. One of the most effective ways to do this is by taking practice tests to evaluate your progress. Practice tests are useful because they show exactly where you need to improve. Every time you take a practice test, pay special attention to these three groups of questions:

- The questions you got wrong
- The questions you had to guess on, even if you guessed right
- The questions you found difficult or slow to work through

This will show you exactly what your weak areas are, and where you need to devote more study time. Ask yourself why each of these questions gave you trouble. Was it because you didn't understand the material? Was it because you didn't remember the vocabulary? Do you need more repetitions on this type of question to build speed and confidence? Dig into those questions and figure out how you can strengthen your weak areas as you go back to review the material.

 Additionally, many practice tests have a section explaining the answer choices. It can be tempting to read the explanation and think that you now have a good understanding of the concept. However, an explanation likely only covers part of the question's broader context. Even if the explanation makes perfect sense, **go back and investigate** every concept related to the question until you're positive you have a thorough understanding.

As you go along, keep in mind that the practice test is just that: practice. Memorizing these questions and answers will not be very helpful on the actual test because it is unlikely to have any of the same exact questions. If you only know the right answers to the sample questions, you won't be prepared for the real thing. **Study the concepts** until you understand them fully, and then you'll be able to answer any question that shows up on the test.

It's important to wait on the practice tests until you're ready. If you take a test on your first day of study, you may be overwhelmed by the amount of material covered and how much you need to learn. Work up to it gradually.

On test day, you'll need to be prepared for answering questions, managing your time, and using the test-taking strategies you've learned. It's a lot to balance, like a mental marathon that will have a big impact on your future. Like training for a marathon, you'll need to start slowly and work your way up. When test day arrives, you'll be ready.

Start with the strategies you've read in the first two Secret Keys—plan your course and study in the way that works best for you. If you have time, consider using multiple study resources to get different approaches to the same concepts. It can be helpful to see difficult concepts from more than one angle. Then find a good source for practice tests. Many times, the test website will suggest potential study resources or provide sample tests.

Practice Test Strategy

If you're able to find at least three practice tests, we recommend this strategy:

UNTIMED AND OPEN-BOOK PRACTICE

Take the first test with no time constraints and with your notes and study guide handy. Take your time and focus on applying the strategies you've learned.

TIMED AND OPEN-BOOK PRACTICE

Take the second practice test open-book as well, but set a timer and practice pacing yourself to finish in time.

TIMED AND CLOSED-BOOK PRACTICE

Take any other practice tests as if it were test day. Set a timer and put away your study materials. Sit at a table or desk in a quiet room, imagine yourself at the testing center, and answer questions as quickly and accurately as possible.

Keep repeating timed and closed-book tests on a regular basis until you run out of practice tests or it's time for the actual test. Your mind will be ready for the schedule and stress of test day, and you'll be able to focus on recalling the material you've learned.

Secret Key #4 – Pace Yourself

Once you're fully prepared for the material on the test, your biggest challenge on test day will be managing your time. Just knowing that the clock is ticking can make you panic even if you have plenty of time left. Work on pacing yourself so you can build confidence against the time constraints of the exam. Pacing is a difficult skill to master, especially in a high-pressure environment, so **practice is vital**.

Set time expectations for your pace based on how much time is available. For example, if a section has 60 questions and the time limit is 30 minutes, you know you have to average 30 seconds or less per question in order to answer them all. Although 30 seconds is the hard limit, set 25 seconds per question as your goal, so you reserve extra time to spend on harder questions. When you budget extra time for the harder questions, you no longer have any reason to stress when those questions take longer to answer.

Don't let this time expectation distract you from working through the test at a calm, steady pace, but keep it in mind so you don't spend too much time on any one question. Recognize that taking extra time on one question you don't understand may keep you from answering two that you do understand later in the test. If your time limit for a question is up and you're still not sure of the answer, mark it and move on, and come back to it later if the time and the test format allow. If the testing format doesn't allow you to return to earlier questions, just make an educated guess; then put it out of your mind and move on.

On the easier questions, be careful not to rush. It may seem wise to hurry through them so you have more time for the challenging ones, but it's not worth missing one if you know the concept and just didn't take the time to read the question fully. Work efficiently but make sure you understand the question and have looked at all of the answer choices, since more than one may seem right at first.

Even if you're paying attention to the time, you may find yourself a little behind at some point. You should speed up to get back on track, but do so wisely. Don't panic; just take a few seconds less on each question until you're caught up. Don't guess without thinking, but do look through the answer choices and eliminate any you know are wrong. If you can get down to two choices, it is often worthwhile to guess from those. Once you've chosen an answer, move on and don't dwell on any that you skipped or had to hurry through. If a question was taking too long, chances are it was one of the harder ones, so you weren't as likely to get it right anyway.

On the other hand, if you find yourself getting ahead of schedule, it may be beneficial to slow down a little. The more quickly you work, the more likely you are to make a careless mistake that will affect your score. You've budgeted time for each question, so don't be afraid to spend that time. Practice an efficient but careful pace to get the most out of the time you have.

Secret Key #5 – Have a Plan for Guessing

When you're taking the test, you may find yourself stuck on a question. Some of the answer choices seem better than others, but you don't see the one answer choice that is obviously correct. What do you do?

The scenario described above is very common, yet most test takers have not effectively prepared for it. Developing and practicing a plan for guessing may be one of the single most effective uses of your time as you get ready for the exam.

In developing your plan for guessing, there are three questions to address:

- When should you start the guessing process?
- How should you narrow down the choices?
- Which answer should you choose?

When to Start the Guessing Process

Unless your plan for guessing is to select C every time (which, despite its merits, is not what we recommend), you need to leave yourself enough time to apply your answer elimination strategies. Since you have a limited amount of time for each question, that means that if you're going to give yourself the best shot at guessing correctly, you have to decide quickly whether or not you will guess.

Of course, the best-case scenario is that you don't have to guess at all, so first, see if you can answer the question based on your knowledge of the subject and basic reasoning skills. Focus on the key words in the question and try to jog your memory of related topics. Give yourself a chance to bring the knowledge to mind, but once you realize that you don't have (or you can't access) the knowledge you need to answer the question, it's time to start the guessing process.

It's almost always better to start the guessing process too early than too late. It only takes a few seconds to remember something and answer the question from knowledge. Carefully eliminating wrong answer choices takes longer. Plus, going through the process of eliminating answer choices can actually help jog your memory.

Summary: Start the guessing process as soon as you decide that you can't answer the question based on your knowledge.

How to Narrow Down the Choices

The next chapter in this book (**Test-Taking Strategies**) includes a wide range of strategies for how to approach questions and how to look for answer choices to eliminate. You will definitely want to read those carefully, practice them, and figure out which ones work best for you. Here though, we're going to address a mindset rather than a particular strategy.

Your odds of guessing an answer correctly depend on how many options you are choosing from.

Number of options left	5	4	3	2	1
Odds of guessing correctly	20%	25%	33%	50%	100%

You can see from this chart just how valuable it is to be able to eliminate incorrect answers and make an educated guess, but there are two things that many test takers do that cause them to miss out on the benefits of guessing:

- Accidentally eliminating the correct answer
- Selecting an answer based on an impression

We'll look at the first one here, and the second one in the next section.

To avoid accidentally eliminating the correct answer, we recommend a thought exercise called **the $5 challenge**. In this challenge, you only eliminate an answer choice from contention if you are willing to bet $5 on it being wrong. Why $5? Five dollars is a small but not insignificant amount of money. It's an amount you could afford to lose but wouldn't want to throw away. And while losing

$5 once might not hurt too much, doing it twenty times will set you back $100. In the same way, each small decision you make—eliminating a choice here, guessing on a question there—won't by itself impact your score very much, but when you put them all together, they can make a big difference. By holding each answer choice elimination decision to a higher standard, you can reduce the risk of accidentally eliminating the correct answer.

The $5 challenge can also be applied in a positive sense: If you are willing to bet $5 that an answer choice *is* correct, go ahead and mark it as correct.

Summary: Only eliminate an answer choice if you are willing to bet $5 that it is wrong.

8

Which Answer to Choose

You're taking the test. You've run into a hard question and decided you'll have to guess. You've eliminated all the answer choices you're willing to bet $5 on. Now you have to pick an answer. Why do we even need to talk about this? Why can't you just pick whichever one you feel like when the time comes?

The answer to these questions is that if you don't come into the test with a plan, you'll rely on your impression to select an answer choice, and if you do that, you risk falling into a trap. The test writers know that everyone who takes their test will be guessing on some of the questions, so they intentionally write wrong answer choices to seem plausible. You still have to pick an answer though, and if the wrong answer choices are designed to look right, how can you ever be sure that you're not falling for their trap? The best solution we've found to this dilemma is to take the decision out of your hands entirely. Here is the process we recommend:

Once you've eliminated any choices that you are confident (willing to bet $5) are wrong, select the first remaining choice as your answer.

Whether you choose to select the first remaining choice, the second, or the last, the important thing is that you use some preselected standard. Using this approach guarantees that you will not be enticed into selecting an answer choice that looks right, because you are not basing your decision on how the answer choices look.

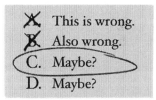

This is not meant to make you question your knowledge. Instead, it is to help you recognize the difference between your knowledge and your impressions. There's a huge difference between thinking an answer is right because of what you know, and thinking an answer is right because it looks or sounds like it should be right.

Summary: To ensure that your selection is appropriately random, make a predetermined selection from among all answer choices you have not eliminated.

Test-Taking Strategies

This section contains a list of test-taking strategies that you may find helpful as you work through the test. By taking what you know and applying logical thought, you can maximize your chances of answering any question correctly!

It is very important to realize that every question is different and every person is different: no single strategy will work on every question, and no single strategy will work for every person. That's why we've included all of them here, so you can try them out and determine which ones work best for different types of questions and which ones work best for you.

Question Strategies

⊘ READ CAREFULLY

Read the question and the answer choices carefully. Don't miss the question because you misread the terms. You have plenty of time to read each question thoroughly and make sure you understand what is being asked. Yet a happy medium must be attained, so don't waste too much time. You must read carefully and efficiently.

⊘ CONTEXTUAL CLUES

Look for contextual clues. If the question includes a word you are not familiar with, look at the immediate context for some indication of what the word might mean. Contextual clues can often give you all the information you need to decipher the meaning of an unfamiliar word. Even if you can't determine the meaning, you may be able to narrow down the possibilities enough to make a solid guess at the answer to the question.

⊘ PREFIXES

If you're having trouble with a word in the question or answer choices, try dissecting it. Take advantage of every clue that the word might include. Prefixes can be a huge help. Usually, they allow you to determine a basic meaning. *Pre-* means before, *post-* means after, *pro-* is positive, *de-* is negative. From prefixes, you can get an idea of the general meaning of the word and try to put it into context.

⊘ HEDGE WORDS

Watch out for critical hedge words, such as *likely, may, can, sometimes, often, almost, mostly, usually, generally, rarely,* and *sometimes.* Question writers insert these hedge phrases to cover every possibility. Often an answer choice will be wrong simply because it leaves no room for exception. Be on guard for answer choices that have definitive words such as *exactly* and *always.*

⊘ SWITCHBACK WORDS

Stay alert for *switchbacks.* These are the words and phrases frequently used to alert you to shifts in thought. The most common switchback words are *but, although,* and *however.* Others include *nevertheless, on the other hand, even though, while, in spite of, despite,* and *regardless of.* Switchback words are important to catch because they can change the direction of the question or an answer choice.

⊘ Face Value

When in doubt, use common sense. Accept the situation in the problem at face value. Don't read too much into it. These problems will not require you to make wild assumptions. If you have to go beyond creativity and warp time or space in order to have an answer choice fit the question, then you should move on and consider the other answer choices. These are normal problems rooted in reality. The applicable relationship or explanation may not be readily apparent, but it is there for you to figure out. Use your common sense to interpret anything that isn't clear.

Answer Choice Strategies

⊘ Answer Selection

The most thorough way to pick an answer choice is to identify and eliminate wrong answers until only one is left, then confirm it is the correct answer. Sometimes an answer choice may immediately seem right, but be careful. The test writers will usually put more than one reasonable answer choice on each question, so take a second to read all of them and make sure that the other choices are not equally obvious. As long as you have time left, it is better to read every answer choice than to pick the first one that looks right without checking the others.

⊘ Answer Choice Families

An answer choice family consists of two (in rare cases, three) answer choices that are very similar in construction and cannot all be true at the same time. If you see two answer choices that are direct opposites or parallels, one of them is usually the correct answer. For instance, if one answer choice says that quantity x increases and another either says that quantity x decreases (opposite) or says that quantity y increases (parallel), then those answer choices would fall into the same family. An answer choice that doesn't match the construction of the answer choice family is more likely to be incorrect. Most questions will not have answer choice families, but when they do appear, you should be prepared to recognize them.

⊘ Eliminate Answers

Eliminate answer choices as soon as you realize they are wrong, but make sure you consider all possibilities. If you are eliminating answer choices and realize that the last one you are left with is also wrong, don't panic. Start over and consider each choice again. There may be something you missed the first time that you will realize on the second pass.

⊘ Avoid Fact Traps

Don't be distracted by an answer choice that is factually true but doesn't answer the question. You are looking for the choice that answers the question. Stay focused on what the question is asking for so you don't accidentally pick an answer that is true but incorrect. Always go back to the question and make sure the answer choice you've selected actually answers the question and is not merely a true statement.

⊘ Extreme Statements

In general, you should avoid answers that put forth extreme actions as standard practice or proclaim controversial ideas as established fact. An answer choice that states the "process should be used in certain situations, if…" is much more likely to be correct than one that states the "process should be discontinued completely." The first is a calm rational statement and doesn't even make a definitive, uncompromising stance, using a hedge word *if* to provide wiggle room, whereas the second choice is far more extreme.

11

⊘ BENCHMARK

As you read through the answer choices and you come across one that seems to answer the question well, mentally select that answer choice. This is not your final answer, but it's the one that will help you evaluate the other answer choices. The one that you selected is your benchmark or standard for judging each of the other answer choices. Every other answer choice must be compared to your benchmark. That choice is correct until proven otherwise by another answer choice beating it. If you find a better answer, then that one becomes your new benchmark. Once you've decided that no other choice answers the question as well as your benchmark, you have your final answer.

⊘ PREDICT THE ANSWER

Before you even start looking at the answer choices, it is often best to try to predict the answer. When you come up with the answer on your own, it is easier to avoid distractions and traps because you will know exactly what to look for. The right answer choice is unlikely to be word-for-word what you came up with, but it should be a close match. Even if you are confident that you have the right answer, you should still take the time to read each option before moving on.

General Strategies

⊘ TOUGH QUESTIONS

If you are stumped on a problem or it appears too hard or too difficult, don't waste time. Move on! Remember though, if you can quickly check for obviously incorrect answer choices, your chances of guessing correctly are greatly improved. Before you completely give up, at least try to knock out a couple of possible answers. Eliminate what you can and then guess at the remaining answer choices before moving on.

⊘ CHECK YOUR WORK

Since you will probably not know every term listed and the answer to every question, it is important that you get credit for the ones that you do know. Don't miss any questions through careless mistakes. If at all possible, try to take a second to look back over your answer selection and make sure you've selected the correct answer choice and haven't made a costly careless mistake (such as marking an answer choice that you didn't mean to mark). This quick double check should more than pay for itself in caught mistakes for the time it costs.

⊘ PACE YOURSELF

It's easy to be overwhelmed when you're looking at a page full of questions; your mind is confused and full of random thoughts, and the clock is ticking down faster than you would like. Calm down and maintain the pace that you have set for yourself. Especially as you get down to the last few minutes of the test, don't let the small numbers on the clock make you panic. As long as you are on track by monitoring your pace, you are guaranteed to have time for each question.

⊘ DON'T RUSH

It is very easy to make errors when you are in a hurry. Maintaining a fast pace in answering questions is pointless if it makes you miss questions that you would have gotten right otherwise. Test writers like to include distracting information and wrong answers that seem right. Taking a little extra time to avoid careless mistakes can make all the difference in your test score. Find a pace that allows you to be confident in the answers that you select.

⊘ Keep Moving

Panicking will not help you pass the test, so do your best to stay calm and keep moving. Taking deep breaths and going through the answer elimination steps you practiced can help to break through a stress barrier and keep your pace.

Final Notes

The combination of a solid foundation of content knowledge and the confidence that comes from practicing your plan for applying that knowledge is the key to maximizing your performance on test day. As your foundation of content knowledge is built up and strengthened, you'll find that the strategies included in this chapter become more and more effective in helping you quickly sift through the distractions and traps of the test to isolate the correct answer.

Now that you're preparing to move forward into the test content chapters of this book, be sure to keep your goal in mind. As you read, think about how you will be able to apply this information on the test. If you've already seen sample questions for the test and you have an idea of the question format and style, try to come up with questions of your own that you can answer based on what you're reading. This will give you valuable practice applying your knowledge in the same ways you can expect to on test day.

Good luck and good studying!

Quantitative Reasoning

BASIC MATHEMATICAL OPERATIONS

There are four basic mathematical operations:

- *Addition* increases the value of one quantity by the value of another quantity. Example: 2 + 4 = 6; 8 + 9 = 17. The result is called the *sum*. With addition, the order does not matter. 4 + 2 = 2 + 4.
- *Subtraction* is the opposite operation of addition; it decreases the value of one quantity by the value of another quantity. Example: 6 – 4 = 2; 17 – 8 = 9. The result is called the *difference*. Note that with subtraction, the order *does* matter. 6 – 4 ≠ 4 – 6.
- *Multiplication* can be thought of as repeated addition. One number tells how many times to add the other number to itself. Example: 3 × 2 (three times two) = 2 + 2 + 2 = 6. With multiplication, the order does not matter. 2 × 3 (or 3 + 3) = 3 × 2 (or 2 + 2 + 2).
- *Division* is the opposite operation of multiplication; one number tells us how many parts to divide the other number into. Example: 20 ÷ 4 = 5; if 20 is split into 4 equal parts, each part is 5. With division, the order of the numbers *does* matter. 20 ÷ 4 ≠ 4 ÷ 20.

> **Review Video: Mathematical Operations**
> Visit mometrix.com/academy and enter code: 208095

COMMON ARITHMETIC TERMS SPECIFIC TO NUMBERS

Numbers are the basic building blocks of mathematics. Specific features of numbers are identified by the following terms:

- *Integers* – The set of positive and negative numbers, including zero. Integers do not include fractions ($\frac{1}{3}$), decimals (0.56), or mixed numbers ($7\frac{3}{4}$).
- *Prime number* – A whole number greater than 1 that has only two factors, itself and 1; that is, a number that can be divided evenly only by 1 and itself.
- *Composite number* – A whole number greater than 1 that has more than two different factors; in other words, any whole number that is not a prime number. For example: The composite number 8 has the factors of 1, 2, 4, and 8.
- *Even number* – Any integer that can be divided by 2 without leaving a remainder. For example: 2, 4, 6, 8, and so on.
- *Odd number* – Any integer that cannot be divided evenly by 2. For example: 3, 5, 7, 9, and so on.

15

RATIONAL, IRRATIONAL, AND REAL NUMBERS

Rational, irrational, and real numbers can be described as follows:

- *Rational numbers* include all integers, decimals, and fractions. Any terminating or repeating decimal number is a rational number.
- *Irrational numbers* cannot be written as fractions or decimals because the number of decimal places is infinite and there is no recurring pattern of digits within the number. For example, pi (π) begins with 3.141592 and continues without terminating or repeating, so pi is an irrational number.
- *Real numbers* are the set of all rational and irrational numbers.

> **Review Video: Classification of Numbers**
> Visit mometrix.com/academy and enter code: 461071
>
> **Review Video: Rational and Irrational Numbers**
> Visit mometrix.com/academy and enter code: 280645
>
> **Review Video: Prime and Composite Numbers**
> Visit mometrix.com/academy and enter code: 565581

FACTORS

Factors are numbers that are multiplied together to obtain a *product*. For example, in the equation $2 \times 3 = 6$, the numbers 2 and 3 are factors. A prime number has only two factors (1 and itself), but other numbers can have many factors.

A *common factor* is a number that divides exactly into two or more other numbers. For example, the factors of 12 are 1, 2, 3, 4, 6, and 12, while the factors of 15 are 1, 3, 5, and 15. The common factors of 12 and 15 are 1 and 3.

A *prime factor* is also a prime number. Therefore, the prime factors of 12 are 2 and 3. For 15, the prime factors are 3 and 5.

> **Review Video: Factors**
> Visit mometrix.com/academy and enter code: 920086

GREATEST COMMON FACTOR (GCF) AND LEAST COMMON MULTIPLE (LCM)

The *greatest common factor* (GCF) is the largest number that is a factor of two or more numbers. For example, the factors of 15 are 1, 3, 5, and 15; the factors of 35 are 1, 5, 7, and 35. Therefore, the greatest common factor of 15 and 35 is 5.

> **Review Video: Greatest Common Factor and Least Common Multiple**
> Visit mometrix.com/academy and enter code: 838699

The *least common multiple* (LCM) is the smallest number that is a multiple of two or more numbers. For example, the multiples of 3 include 3, 6, 9, 12, 15, etc.; the multiples of 5 include 5, 10, 15, 20, etc. Therefore, the least common multiple of 3 and 5 is 15.

FINDING THE GREATEST COMMON FACTOR OF A GROUP OF ALGEBRAIC EXPRESSIONS

The greatest common factor of a group of algebraic expressions may be a *monomial* or a *polynomial*. Begin by factoring all the algebraic expressions until each expression is represented as a group of

16

factors consisting of monomials and prime polynomials. To find the greatest common factor, take each monomial or polynomial that appear as a factor in every algebraic expression and multiply. This will give you a polynomial with the largest numerical coefficient and largest degree that is a factor of the given algebraic expressions.

SCIENTIFIC NOTATION

Scientific notation is a way of writing large numbers in a shorter form. The form a × 10^n is used in scientific notation, where a is greater than or equal to 1, but less than 10, and n is the number of places the decimal must move to get from the original number to a.

Example: The number 230,400,000 is cumbersome to write. To write the value in scientific notation, place a decimal point between the first and second numbers, and include all digits through the last non-zero digit (a = 2.304). To find the appropriate power of 10, count the number of places the decimal point had to move (n = 8). The number is positive if the decimal moved to the left, and negative if it moved to the right. We can then write 230,400,000 as $2.304 × 10^8$.

If we look instead at the number 0.00002304, we have the same value for a, but this time the decimal moved 5 places to the right (n = -5). Thus, 0.00002304 can be written as $2.304 × 10^{-5}$. Using this notation makes it simple to compare very large or very small numbers. By comparing exponents, it is easy to see that $3.28 × 10^4$ is smaller than $1.51 × 10^5$, because 4 is less than 5.

Review Video: <u>Scientific Notation</u>
Visit mometrix.com/academy and enter code: 976454

LAWS OF EXPONENTS

The laws of exponents are as follows:

1. Any number to the power of 1 is equal to itself: $a^1 = a$.
2. The number 1 raised to any power is equal to 1: $1^n = 1$.
3. Any number raised to the power of 0 is equal to 1: $a^0 = 1$.
4. Add exponents to multiply powers of the same base number: $a^n × a^m = a^{n+m}$.
5. Subtract exponents to divide powers of the same number: $a^n ÷ a^m = a^{n-m}$.
6. Multiply exponents to raise a power to a power: $(a^n)^m = a^{n×m}$.
7. If multiplied or divided numbers inside parentheses are collectively raised to a power, this is the same as each individual term being raised to that power: $(a × b)^n = a^n × b^n$; $(a ÷ b)^n = a^n ÷ b^n$.

Note: Exponents do not have to be integers. Fractional or decimal exponents follow all the rules above as well. Example: $5^{\frac{1}{4}} × 5^{\frac{3}{4}} = 5^{\frac{1}{4}+\frac{3}{4}} = 5^1 = 5$.

Review Video: <u>Properties of Exponents</u>
Visit mometrix.com/academy and enter code: 532558

DECIMAL SYSTEM

The decimal, or base 10, system is a number system that uses ten different digits (0, 1, 2, 3, 4, 5, 6, 7, 8, 9). An example of a number system that uses something other than ten digits is the binary, or

Quantitative Reasoning

17

base 2, number system, used by computers, which uses only the numbers 0 and 1. It is thought that the decimal system originated because people had only their 10 fingers for counting.

- *Decimal* – a number that uses a decimal point to show the part of the number that is less than one. Example: 1.234.
- *Decimal point* – a symbol used to separate the ones place from the tenths place in decimals or dollars from cents in currency.
- *Decimal place* – the position of a number to the right of the decimal point. In the decimal 0.123, the 1 is in the first place to the right of the decimal point, indicating tenths; the 2 is in the second place, indicating hundredths; and the 3 is in the third place, indicating thousandths.

> **Review Video: Decimals**
> Visit mometrix.com/academy and enter code: 837268

STANDARD UNITS IN THE METRIC SYSTEM COMPARED TO THE U.S. CUSTOMARY SYSTEM
METRIC SYSTEM

- Length: meter
- Mass or weight: gram
- Volume: liter
- Temperature: degrees Celsius

U.S. CUSTOMARY SYSTEM

- Length: inch, foot, yard, mile
- Capacity or volume: pint, quart, gallon
- Mass or weight: ounce, pound, ton
- Temperature: degrees Fahrenheit

COMMON CONVERSIONS FOR LENGTH IN THE U.S. CUSTOMARY SYSTEM

- 1 foot = 12 inches
- 1 yard = 3 feet
- 1 mile = 5,280 feet

COMMON PREFIXES USED IN THE METRIC SYSTEM

- *Milli* – one one-thousandth, or .001
- *Centi* – one one-hundredth, or .01
- *Kilo* – one thousand, or 1,000

COMMON CONVERSIONS FOR LIQUID CAPACITY IN THE U.S. CUSTOMARY SYSTEM

- 1 cup = 8 fluid ounces
- 1 pint = 2 cups
- 1 quart = 2 pints
- 1 gallon = 4 quarts

Quantitative Reasoning

COMMON CONVERSIONS FOR WEIGHT IN THE U.S. CUSTOMARY SYSTEM

- 1 pound = 16 ounces
- 1 ton = 2,000 pounds

> **Review Video: Metric System Conversions**
> Visit mometrix.com/academy and enter code: 163709

FRACTIONS, NUMERATORS, AND DENOMINATORS

A *fraction* is a number that is expressed as one integer written above another integer, with a dividing line between them $\left(\frac{x}{y}\right)$. It represents the quotient of the two numbers "x divided by y." It can also be thought of as x out of y equal parts.

The top number of a fraction is called the *numerator*, and it represents the number of parts under consideration. The 1 in $\frac{1}{4}$ means that 1 part out of the whole is being considered in the calculation. The bottom number of a fraction is called the *denominator*, and it represents the total number of equal parts. The 4 in $\frac{1}{4}$ means that the whole consists of 4 equal parts.

A fraction cannot have a denominator of zero; this is referred to as "undefined."

> **Review Video: Overview of Fractions**
> Visit mometrix.com/academy and enter code: 262335

MANIPULATING FRACTIONS

Fractions can be manipulated by multiplying or dividing (but not adding or subtracting) both the numerator and denominator by the same number, without changing the value of the fraction. If you divide both numbers by a common factor, you are reducing or simplifying the fraction. Two fractions that have the same value, but are expressed differently are known as *equivalent fractions*. For example, $\frac{2}{10}, \frac{3}{15}, \frac{4}{20}$, and $\frac{5}{25}$ are all equivalent fractions. They can also all be reduced or simplified to $\frac{1}{5}$.

When two fractions are manipulated so that they have the same denominator, this is known as finding a *common denominator*. The number chosen to be that common denominator should be the least common multiple of the two original denominators. Example: $\frac{3}{4}$ and $\frac{5}{6}$; the least common multiple of 4 and 6 is 12. Manipulating to achieve the common denominator: $\frac{3}{4} = \frac{9}{12}$; $\frac{5}{6} = \frac{10}{12}$.

IMPROPER FRACTIONS AND MIXED NUMBERS

A fraction whose denominator is greater than its numerator is known as a *proper fraction*, while a fraction whose numerator is greater than its denominator is known as an *improper fraction*. Proper fractions have values less than one while improper fractions have values greater than one.

A *mixed number* is a number that contains both an integer and a fraction. Any improper fraction can be rewritten as a mixed number. Example: $\frac{8}{3} = \frac{6}{3} + \frac{2}{3} = 2 + \frac{2}{3} = 2\frac{2}{3}$. Similarly, any mixed number can be rewritten as an improper fraction. Example: $1\frac{3}{5} = 1 + \frac{3}{5} = \frac{5}{5} + \frac{3}{5} = \frac{8}{5}$.

> **Review Video: Improper Fractions and Mixed Numbers**
> Visit mometrix.com/academy and enter code: 211077

ADDING, SUBTRACTING, MULTIPLYING, AND DIVIDING FRACTIONS

If two fractions have a common denominator, they can be added or subtracted simply by adding or subtracting the two numerators and retaining the same denominator. Example: $\frac{1}{2} + \frac{1}{4} = \frac{2}{4} + \frac{1}{4} = \frac{3}{4}$. If the two fractions do not already have the same denominator, one or both of them must be manipulated to achieve a common denominator before they can be added or subtracted.

> **Review Video: Adding and Subtracting Fractions**
> Visit mometrix.com/academy and enter code: 378080

Two fractions can be multiplied by multiplying the two numerators to find the new numerator and the two denominators to find the new denominator. Example: $\frac{1}{3} \times \frac{2}{3} = \frac{1\times2}{3\times3} = \frac{2}{9}$.

Two fractions can be divided flipping the numerator and denominator of the second fraction and then proceeding as though it were a multiplication. Example: $\frac{2}{3} \div \frac{3}{4} = \frac{2}{3} \times \frac{4}{3} = \frac{8}{9}$.

> **Review Video: Multiplying and Dividing Fractions**
> Visit mometrix.com/academy and enter code: 473632

COMPLEX FRACTIONS

Complex fraction: A fraction that contains a fraction in its numerator, denominator, or both. These can be solved in a number of ways, with the simplest being by following the order of operations.

For example, $\frac{\left(\frac{4}{7}\right)}{\left(\frac{5}{8}\right)} = \frac{0.571}{0.625} = 0.914$.

Another way to solve this problem is to multiply the fraction in the numerator by the reciprical of the fraction in the denominator. For example, $\frac{\left(\frac{4}{7}\right)}{\left(\frac{5}{8}\right)} = \frac{4}{7} \times \frac{8}{5} = \frac{32}{35} = 0.914$.

PERCENTAGES, FRACTIONS, AND DECIMALS

Percentages can be thought of as fractions that are based on a whole of 100; that is, one whole is equal to 100%. The word percent means *per hundred*. Fractions can be expressed as percents by finding equivalent fractions with a denomination of 100. Example: $\frac{7}{10} = \frac{70}{100} = 70\%; \frac{1}{4} = \frac{25}{100} = 25\%$.

To express a percentage as a fraction, divide the percentage number by 100 and reduce the fraction to its simplest possible terms. Example: $60\% = \frac{60}{100} = \frac{3}{5}; 96\% = \frac{96}{100} = \frac{24}{25}$.

Converting decimals to percentages and percentages to decimals is as simple as moving the decimal point. To convert from a decimal to a percent, move the decimal point two places to the right. To convert from a percent to a decimal, move it two places to the left. Example: 0.23 = 23%; 5.34 = 534%; 0.007 = 0.7%; 700% = 7.00; 86% = 0.86; 0.15% = 0.0015.

It may be helpful to remember that the percentage number will always be larger than the equivalent decimal number.

PERCENTAGE PROBLEMS

A percentage problem can be presented three main ways:

- Find what percentage of some number another number is. Example: What percentage of 40 is 8?
- Find what number is some percentage of a given number. Example: What number is 20% of 40?
- Find what number another number is a given percentage of. Example: What number is 8 20% of?

The three components in all of these cases are the same: a *whole* (W), a *part* (P), and a *percentage* (%). These are related by the equation:

- $P = W \times \%$. This is the form of the equation you would use to solve problems of type (2). To solve types (1) and (3), you would use these two forms: $\% = P/W$ and $W = P/\%$.

The thing that frequently makes percentage problems difficult is that they are often also word problems, so a large part of solving them is figuring out which quantities are what. Example: In a school cafeteria, 7 students choose pizza, 9 choose hamburgers, and 4 choose tacos. Find the percentage that chooses tacos. To find the whole, you must first add all of the parts: 7 + 9 + 4 = 20. The percentage can then be found by dividing the part by the whole ($\% = P/W$): $\frac{4}{20} = \frac{20}{100} = 20\%$.

RATIO AND PROPORTION

A *ratio* is a comparison of two quantities in a particular order. Example: if there are 14 computers in a lab, and the class has 20 students, there is a student to computer ratio of 20 to 14, commonly written as 20:14.

A proportion is a relationship between two quantities that dictates how one changes when the other changes. A *direct proportion* describes a relationship in which a quantity increases by a set amount for every increase in the other quantity, or decreases by that same amount for every decrease in the other quantity. Example: For every 1 sheet cake, 18 people can be served cake. The number of sheet cakes, and the number of people that can be served from them is directly proportional.

An **inverse proportion** is a relationship in which an increase in one quantity is accompanied by a decrease in the other, or vice versa. Example: the time required for a car trip decreases as the speed increases, and increases as the speed decreases, so the time required is inversely proportional to the speed of the car.

DISTANCE, RATE, AND TIME

Distance is achieved by moving at a given rate for a given length of time. The formulas that relate the three are

- $d = rt$, $r = \frac{d}{t}$, and $t = \frac{d}{r}$, where d is the distance, r is the rate of change over time, and t is total time.

In these formulas, the units used to express the rate must be the same units used to express the distance and the time.

21

EXPONENTS AND PARENTHESES

An *exponent* is a superscript number placed next to another number at the top right. It indicates how many times the base number is to be multiplied by itself. Exponents provide a shorthand way to write what would be a longer mathematical expression. Example: $a^2 = a \times a$; $2^4 = 2 \times 2 \times 2 \times 2$. A number with an exponent of 2 is said to be "squared," while a number with an exponent of 3 is said to be "cubed." The value of a number raised to an exponent is called its *power*. So, 8^4 is read as "8 to the 4th power," or "8 raised to the power of 4." A *negative exponent* is the same as the reciprocal of a positive exponent. Example: $a^{-2} = 1/a^2$.

> **Review Video: Exponents**
> Visit mometrix.com/academy and enter code: 600998

Parentheses are used to designate which operations should be done first when there are multiple operations. Example: $4 - (2 + 1) = 1$; the parentheses tell us that we must add 2 and 1, and then subtract the sum from 4, rather than subtracting 2 from 4 and then adding 1 (this would give us an answer of 3).

RATIONAL EXPRESSIONS

Rational expression: A fraction with polynomials in both the numerator and the denominator; the value of the polynomial in the denominator cannot be equal to zero.

To add or subtract rational expressions, first find the common denominator, then rewrite each fraction as an equivalent fraction with the common denominator. Finally, add or subtract the numerators to get the numerator of the answer, and keep the common denominator as the denominator of the answer.

When multiplying rational expressions, factor each polynomial and cancel like factors (a factor which appears in both the numerator and the denominator). Then, multiply all remaining factors in the numerator to get the numerator of the product, and multiply the remaining factors in the denominator to get the denominator of the product. Remember – cancel entire factors, not individual terms.

To divide rational expressions, take the reciprocal of the divisor (the rational expression you are dividing by) and multiply by the dividend.

> **Review Video: Rational Expressions**
> Visit mometrix.com/academy and enter code: 415183

ORDER OF OPERATIONS AND PEMDAS

Order of Operations is a set of rules that dictates the order in which we must perform each operation in an expression so that we will evaluate it accurately. If we have an expression that includes multiple different operations, Order of Operations tells us which operations to do first. The most common mnemonic for Order of Operations is *PEMDAS*, or ***Please Excuse My Dear Aunt Sally***. PEMDAS stands for *Parentheses, Exponents, Multiplication, Division, Addition, Subtraction*. It is important to understand that multiplication and division have equal precedence, as do addition and subtraction, so those pairs of operations are simply worked from left to right in order.

Quantitative Reasoning

Example: Evaluate the expression $5 + 20 \div 4 \times (2 + 3)^2 - 6$ using the correct order of operations.

- **P:** Perform the operations inside the parentheses: $(2 + 3) = 5$
- **E:** Simplify the exponents: $(5)^2 = 5 \times 5 = 25$
  - The expression now looks like this: $5 + 20 \div 4 \times 25 - 6$
- **MD:** Perform multiplication and division from left to right: $20 \div 4 = 5$; then $5 \times 25 = 125$
  - The expression now looks like this: $5 + 125 - 6$
- **AS:** Perform addition and subtraction from left to right: $5 + 125 = 130$; then $130 - 6 = 124$

> **Review Video: <u>Order of Operations</u>**
> Visit mometrix.com/academy and enter code: 259675

SYSTEMS OF EQUATIONS

System of equations: A set of simultaneous equations that all use the same variables. A solution to a system of equations must be true for each equation in the system.

Consistent system: A system of equations that has at least one solution.

Inconsistent System: A system of equations that has no solution.

Systems of equations may be solved using one of four methods: substitution, elimination, transformation of the augmented matrix and using the trace feature on a graphing calculator.

> **Review Video: <u>Solving Linear Equations</u>**
> Visit mometrix.com/academy and enter code: 746745
>
> **Review Video: <u>Top 3 Methods for Solving Systems of Equations</u>**
> Visit mometrix.com/academy and enter code: 281590

EQUATIONS

Equation: States that two mathematical expressions are equal.

One Variable Linear Equation: An equation written in the form $ax + b = 0$, where $a \neq 0$.

Root: A solution to a one-variable equation; a number that makes the equation true when it is substituted for the variable.

Solution Set: The set of all solutions of an equation.

Empty Set: A situation in which an equation has no true solution.

Equivalent Equations: Equations with identical solution sets.

> **Review Video: <u>Equations and Inequalities</u>**
> Visit mometrix.com/academy and enter code: 869843

SOLVING ONE-VARIABLE LINEAR EQUATIONS

Multiply all terms by the lowest common denominator to eliminate any fractions. Look for addition or subtraction to undo so you can isolate the variable on one side of the equal sign. Divide both sides by the coefficient of the variable. When you have a value for the variable, substitute this value into the original equation to make sure you have a true equation.

DIFFERENT FORMS OF LINEAR EQUATIONS

Linear equations can be written in three different forms, each used for a different purpose. The standard form of linear equations is $Ax + By = C$, where A, B and C are integers and A is a positive number. Any equation can be written in this form. This is helpful in solving and graphing systems of equations, where you must compare two or more equations. You can graph an equation in standard form by finding the intercepts. Determine the x-intercept by substituting zero in for y and vice versa. Next, the slope-intercept form of an equation is $y = mx + b$, where m is equal to the slope and b is equal to the y-intercept. You can graph an equation in this form by first plotting the y-intercept. If b is -2, you know that the y-intercept is equal to $(0, -2)$. From this point you can use the slope to create an additional point. If the slope is 4, or $\frac{4}{1}$, you would rise, or move up 4 units and run, or move over 1 unit from the y-intercept. Finally, the point-slope form of an equation is useful when you know the slope and a point on the line. It is written as $y - y_1 = m(x - x_1)$, where m is equal to the slope and (x_1, y_1) is a point on the line. You can graph an equation in point-slope form by plotting the given point and using the slope to plot additional points on the line.

> **Review Video: Linear Equations Basics**
> Visit mometrix.com/academy and enter code: 793005

QUADRATIC FORMULA

The *quadratic formula* is used to solve quadratic equations when other methods are more difficult. To use the quadratic formula to solve a quadratic equation, begin by rewriting the equation in standard form $ax^2 + bx + c = 0$, where a, b, and c are coefficients. Once you have identified the values of the coefficients, substitute those values into the quadratic formula $= \frac{-b \pm \sqrt{b^2 - 4ac}}{2a}$.

Evaluate the equation and simplify the expression. Again, check each root by substituting into the original equation. In the quadratic formula, the portion of the formula under the radical $(b^2 - 4ac)$ is called the *discriminant*. If the discriminant is zero, there is only one root: zero. If the discriminant is positive, there are two different real roots. If the discriminant is negative, there are no real roots.

> **Review Video: Using the Quadratic Formula**
> Visit mometrix.com/academy and enter code: 163102

ONE-VARIABLE QUADRATIC EQUATIONS

One-Variable Quadratic Equation: An equation that can be written in the form $x^2 + bx + c = 0$, where a, b, and c are the coefficients. This is also known as the standard form of an equation.

The solutions of quadratic equations are called *roots*. A quadratic equation may have one real root, two different real roots, or no real roots. The roots can be found using one of three methods: factoring, completing the square, or using the quadratic formula.

Any time you are solving a quadratic equation, never divide both sides by the variable or any expression containing the variable. You are at risk of dividing by zero if you do, thus getting an extraneous, or invalid, root.

SOLVING QUADRATIC EQUATIONS BY FACTORING

Begin by rewriting the equation in standard form, if necessary. Factor the side with the variable. Set each of the factors equal to zero and solve the resulting linear equations. Check your answers by substituting the roots you found into the original equation.

If, when writing the equation in standard form, you have an equation in the form $x^2 + c = 0$ or $x^2 - c = 0$, set $x^2 = -c$ or $x^2 = c$ and take the square root of c. If $c = 0$, the only real root is zero. If c is positive, there are two real roots—the positive and negative square root values. If c is negative, there are no real roots because you cannot take the square root of a negative number.

COMPLETING THE SQUARE TO SOLVE A QUADRATIC EQUATION

To complete the square, rewrite the equation so that all terms containing the variable are on the left side of the equal sign, and all the constants are on the right side of the equal sign. Make sure the coefficient of the squared term is 1. If there is a coefficient with the squared term, divide each term on both sides of the equal side by that number. Next, work with the coefficient of the single-variable term. Square half of this coefficient, and add that value to both sides. Now you can factor the left side (the side containing the variable) as the square of a binomial. $x^2 + 2ax + a^2 = C \Rightarrow (x + a)^2 = C$, where x is the variable, and a and C are constants. Take the square root of both sides and solve for the variable. Substitute the value of the variable in the original problem to check your work.

SOLVING SYSTEMS OF TWO LINEAR EQUATIONS BY SUBSTITUTION

To solve a system of linear equations by substitution, start with the easier equation and solve for one of the variables. Express this variable in terms of the other variable. Substitute this expression into the other equation, and solve for the other variable. The solution should be expressed in the form (x, y). Substitute the values into both of the original equations to check your answer.

EXAMPLE

Solve the following system using substitution:

$$x + 6y = 15$$
$$3x - 12y = 18$$

Solve the first equation for x:

$$x = 15 - 6y$$

Substitute this value in place of x in the second equation, and solve for y:

$$3(15 - 6y) - 12y = 18$$
$$45 - 18y - 12y = 18$$
$$30y = 27$$

$$y = \frac{27}{30} = \frac{9}{10} = 0.9$$

Plug this value for y back into the first equation to solve for x:

$$x = 15 - 6(0.9) = 15 - 5.4 = 9.6$$

SOLVING SYSTEMS OF TWO LINEAR EQUATIONS BY ELIMINATION

To solve a system of equations using elimination, begin by rewriting both equations in standard form $Ax + By = C$. Check to see if the coefficients of one pair of like variables adds to zero. If not, multiply one or both of the equations by a non-zero number to make one set of like variables add to zero. Add the two equations to solve for one of the variables. Substitute back into either original equation to solve for the other variable. Check your work by substituting into the other equation.

> **Review Video: The Elimination Method**
> Visit mometrix.com/academy and enter code: 449121

EXAMPLE

Solve the system using elimination:

$$x + 6y = 15$$

$$3x - 12y = 18$$

If we multiply the first equation by 2, we can eliminate the y terms:

$$2x + 12y = 30$$

$$3x - 12y = 18$$

Add the equations together and solve for x:

$$5x = 48$$

$$x = \frac{48}{5} = 9.6$$

Plug value for x back into either of the original equations and solve for y:

$$9.6 + 6y = 15$$

$$y = \frac{15 - 9.6}{6} = 0.9$$

MONOMIALS AND POLYNOMIALS

Monomial: A single constant, variable, or product of constants and variables, such as 2, x, $2x$, or $\frac{2}{x}$. There will never be addition or subtraction symbols in a monomial. Like monomials have like variables, but they may have different coefficients.

Polynomial: An algebraic expression which uses addition and subtraction to combine two or more monomials. Two terms make a binomial; three terms make a trinomial.

Review Video: Intro to Polynomials
Visit mometrix.com/academy and enter code: 413222

Review Video: Polynomials
Visit mometrix.com/academy and enter code: 305005

Degree of a Monomial: The sum of the exponents of the variables.

Degree of a Polynomial: The highest degree of any individual term.

DIVIDING POLYNOMIALS

Use long division to divide a polynomial by either a monomial or another polynomial of equal or lesser degree. When **dividing by a monomial**, divide each term of the polynomial by the monomial. When **dividing by a polynomial**, begin by arranging the terms of each polynomial in order of one variable. You may arrange in ascending or descending order, but be consistent with both polynomials. To get the first term of the quotient, divide the first term of the dividend by the first term of the divisor. Multiply the first term of the quotient by the entire divisor and subtract that product from the dividend. Repeat for the second and successive terms until you either get a remainder of zero or a remainder whose degree is less than the degree of the divisor. If the quotient has a remainder, write the answer as a mixed expression in the form: quotient $+ \frac{\text{remainder}}{\text{divisor}}$

FACTORING A POLYNOMIAL

First, check for a common monomial factor. When the greatest common monomial factor has been factored out, look for patterns of special products: differences of two squares, the sum or difference of two cubes for binomial factors, or perfect trinomial squares for trinomial factors. If the factor is a trinomial but not a perfect trinomial square, look for a factorable form, such as

$x^2 + (a + b)x + ab = (x + a)(x + b)$ or

$(ac)x^2 + (ad + bc)x + bd = (ax + b)(cx + d)$.

For factors with four terms, look for groups to factor. Once you have found the factors, write the original polynomial as the product of all the factors. Make sure all of the polynomial factors are prime. Monomial factors may be prime or composite. Check your work by multiplying the factors to make sure you get the original polynomial.

MEAN AND WEIGHTED MEAN

Mean: The same thing as the arithmetic average. Use the formula

$$\text{mean} = \frac{\text{sum of all numbers in the set}}{\text{quantity of numbers in the set}}$$

Review Video: Mean, Median, and Mode
Visit mometrix.com/academy and enter code: 286207

Weighted mean: Weighted values, such as $w_1, w_2, w_3, \dots$ are assigned to each member of the set $x_1, x_2, x_3, \dots$. Use the formula

Quantitative Reasoning

Copyright © Mometrix Media. You have been licensed one copy of this document for personal use only. Any other reproduction or redistribution is strictly prohibited. All rights reserved.
This content is provided for test preparation purposes only and does not imply an endorsement by Mometrix of any particular political, scientific, or religious point of view.

$$\text{weighted mean} = \frac{w_1x_1 + w_2x_2 + w_3x_3 + \cdots + w_nx_n}{w_1 + w_2 + w_3 + \cdots + w_n}$$

Make sure there is one weighted value for each member of the set.

PERFECT TRINOMIAL SQUARES, THE DIFFERENCE BETWEEN TWO SQUARES, THE SUM AND DIFFERENCE OF TWO CUBES, AND PERFECT CUBES

Perfect trinomial squares: $x^2 + 2xy + y^2 = (x + y)^2$ or $x^2 - 2xy + y^2 = (x - y)^2$

Difference between two squares: $x^2 - y^2 = (x + y)(x - y)$

Sum of two cubes: $x^3 + y^3 = (x + y)(x^2 - xy + y^2)$

Note: the second factor is **not** the same as a perfect trinomial square, so do not try to factor it further.

Difference between two cubes: $x^3 - y^3 = (x - y)(x^2 + xy + y^2)$ Again, the second factor is **not** the same as a perfect trinomial square.

Perfect cubes: $x^3 + 3x^2y + 3xy^2 + y^3 = (x + y)^3$ and

$$x^3 - 3x^2y + 3xy^2 - y^3 = (x - y)^3$$

MULTIPLYING TWO BINOMIALS

F = **F**irst: Multiply the first term of each binomial
O = **O**uter: Multiply the outer terms of the binomials
I = **I**nner: Multiply the inner terms of the binomials
L = **L**ast: Multiply the last term of each binomial

$$(Ax + By)(Cx + Dy) = ACx^2 + ADxy + BCxy + BDy^2$$

SLOPE, HORIZONTAL, VERTICAL, PARALLEL, PERPENDICULAR

Slope: A ratio of the change in height to the change in horizontal distance. On a graph with two points (x_1, y_1) and (x_2, y_2), the slope is represented by the formula $m = \frac{y_2 - y_1}{x_2 - x_1}$; $x_1 \neq x_2$. If the value of the slope is positive, the line slopes upward from left to right. If the value of the slope is negative, the line slopes downward from left to right. If the y-coordinates are the same for both points, the slope is 0 and the line is a horizontal line. If the x-coordinates are the same for both points, there is no slope and the line is a vertical line.

Horizontal: Having a slope of zero. On a graph, a line that is the same distance from the x-axis at all points.

Vertical: Having no slope. On a graph, a line that is the same distance from the y-axis at all points.

Parallel: Lines that have equal slopes.

Perpendicular: Lines that have slopes that are negative reciprocals of each other: $\frac{a}{b}$ and $\frac{-b}{a}$.

STATISTICS

Statistics may be descriptive or inferential, in nature. Descriptive statistics does not involve inferences and includes measures of center and spread, frequencies, and percentages. Inferential statistics

Quantitative Reasoning

involves the process of making inferences about large populations based on the characteristics of random samples from the population. This field of statistics is useful because, for large populations, it may be impractical or impossible to measure the characteristics of each element of the population and determine the distributions of various properties exactly. By applying statistical methods, it's possible to make reasonable inferences about the distributions of a variable, or variables, throughout large populations by only examining a relatively small part of it. Of course, it's important that this be a "representative sample", that is, one in which the distribution of the variables of interest is similar to its distribution in the entire population. For this reason, it's desirable to create random samples, rather than choosing a set of similar samples.

CONDITIONAL PROBABILITY

Given two events A and B, the **conditional probability** $P(A|B)$ is the probability that event A will occur, given that event B has occurred. For instance, suppose you have a jar containing two red marbles and two blue marbles, and you draw two marbles at random. Note. The first drawn marble is not replaced. Consider event A being the event that the first marble drawn is red, and event B being the event that the *second* marble drawn is blue. With no conditions set, both $P(A)$ and $P(B)$ are equal to $\frac{1}{2}$. However, if we know that the first marble drawn was red—that is, that event A occurred—then that leaves one red marble and two blue marbles in the jar. In that case, the probability that the second marble is blue *given that the first marble was red*—that is, $P(A|B)$—is equal to $\frac{2}{3}$.

CALCULATING THE CONDITIONAL PROBABILITY $P(A|B)$ IN TERMS OF THE PROBABILITIES OF EVENTS A AND B AND THEIR UNION AND/OR INTERSECTION

The conditional probability $P(A|B)$ is the probability that event B will occur given that event A occurs. This cannot be calculated simply from $P(A)$ and $P(B)$; these probabilities alone do not give sufficient information to determine the conditional probability. It can, however, be determined given also $P(A \cap B)$, the probability that events A and B both occur. Specifically, $P(A|B) = \frac{P(A\cap B)}{P(B)}$.

For instance, suppose you have a jar containing two red marbles and two blue marbles, and you draw two marbles at random. Consider event A being the event that the first marble drawn is red, and event B being the event that the *second* marble drawn is blue. $P(A)$ is $\frac{1}{2}$, and $P(A \cap B)$ is $\frac{1}{3}$. (The latter may not be obvious, but may be determined by finding the product of $\frac{1}{2}$ and $\frac{2}{3}$.) Therefore, $P(A|B) = \frac{1/3}{1/2} = \frac{2}{3}$.

Verbal Reasoning

EXPOSITORY PASSAGE

An **expository** passage aims to inform and enlighten readers. The passage is nonfiction and usually centers around a simple, easily defined topic. Since the goal of exposition is to teach, such a passage should be as clear as possible. Often, an expository passage contains helpful organizing words, like *first*, *next*, *for example*, and *therefore*. These words keep the reader oriented in the text. Although expository passages do not need to feature colorful language and artful writing, they are often more effective with these features. For a reader, the challenge of expository passages is to maintain steady attention. Expository passages are not always about subjects that will naturally interest a reader, and the writer is often more concerned with clarity and comprehensibility than with engaging the reader. By reading actively, you will ensure a good habit of focus when reading an expository passage.

> **Review Video: Expository Passages**
> Visit mometrix.com/academy and enter code: 256515

TECHNICAL PASSAGE

A **technical** passage is written to describe a complex object or process. Technical writing is common in medical and technological fields, in which complex ideas of mathematics, science, and engineering need to be explained simply and clearly. To ease comprehension, a technical passage usually proceeds in a very logical order. Technical passages often have clear headings and subheadings, which are used to keep the reader oriented in the text. Additionally, you will find that these passages divide sections up with numbers or letters. Many technical passages look more like an outline than a piece of prose. The amount of jargon or difficult vocabulary will vary in a technical passage depending on the intended audience. As much as possible, technical passages try to avoid language that the reader will have to research in order to understand the message, yet readers will find that jargon cannot always be avoided.

> **Review Video: Technical Passages**
> Visit mometrix.com/academy and enter code: 478923

INFORMATIVE TEXT

An **informative text** is written to educate and enlighten readers. Informative texts are almost always nonfiction and are rarely structured as a story. The intention of an informative text is to deliver information in the most comprehensible way. So, look for the structure of the text to be very clear. In an informative text, the thesis statement is one or two sentences that normally appears at the end of the first paragraph. The author may use some colorful language, but he or she is likely to put more emphasis on clarity and precision. Informative essays do not typically appeal to the emotions. They often contain facts and figures and rarely include the opinion of the author; however, readers should remain aware of the possibility for a bias as those facts are presented. Sometimes a persuasive essay can resemble an informative essay, especially if the author maintains an even tone and presents his or her views as if they were established fact.

> **Review Video: Informative Text**
> Visit mometrix.com/academy and enter code: 924964

DESCRIPTIVE TEXT

In a sense, almost all writing is descriptive, insofar as an author seeks to describe events, ideas, or people to the reader. Some texts, however, are primarily concerned with **description**. A descriptive text focuses on a particular subject and attempts to depict the subject in a way that will be clear to readers. Descriptive texts contain many adjectives and adverbs (i.e., words that give shades of meaning and create a more detailed mental picture for the reader). A descriptive text fails when it is unclear to the reader. A descriptive text will certainly be informative and may be persuasive and entertaining as well.

> **Review Video: Descriptive Texts**
> Visit mometrix.com/academy and enter code: 174903

IDENTIFYING AN AUTHOR'S PURPOSE

Usually, identifying the **purpose** of an author is easier than identifying his or her position. In most cases, the author has no interest in hiding his or her purpose. A text that is meant to entertain, for instance, should be written to please the reader. Most narratives, or stories, are written to entertain, though they may also inform or persuade. Informative texts are easy to identify, while the most difficult purpose of a text to identify is persuasion because the author has an interest in making this purpose hard to detect. When a reader discovers that the author is trying to persuade, he or she should be skeptical of the argument. For this reason, persuasive texts often try to establish an entertaining tone and hope to amuse the reader into agreement. On the other hand, an informative tone may be implemented to create an appearance of authority and objectivity.

An author's purpose is evident often in the organization of the text (e.g., section headings in bold font points to an informative text). However, you may not have such organization available to you in your exam. Instead, if the author makes his or her main idea clear from the beginning, then the likely purpose of the text is to inform. If the author begins by making a claim and provides various arguments to support that claim, then the purpose is probably to persuade. If the author tells a story or seems to want the attention of the reader more than to push a particular point or deliver information, then his or her purpose is most likely to entertain. As a reader, you must judge authors on how well they accomplish their purpose. In other words, you need to consider the type of passage (e.g., technical, persuasive, etc.) that the author has written and whether the author has followed the requirements of the passage type.

COMPARING AND CONTRASTING

Authors will use different stylistic and writing devices to make their meaning clear for readers. One of those devices is comparison and contrast. As mentioned previously, when an author describes the ways in which two things are alike, he or she is **comparing** them. When the author describes the ways in which two things are different, he or she is **contrasting** them. The "compare and contrast" essay is one of the most common forms in nonfiction. These passages are often signaled with certain words: a comparison may have indicating terms such as *both, same, like, too,* and *as well*; while a contrast may have terms like *but, however, on the other hand, instead,* and *yet*. Of course, comparisons and contrasts may be implicit without using any such signaling language. A single sentence may both compare and contrast. Consider the sentence *Brian and Sheila love ice cream, but Brian prefers vanilla and Sheila prefers strawberry*. In one sentence, the author has described both a similarity (love of ice cream) and a difference (favorite flavor).

> **Review Video: Compare and Contrast**
> Visit mometrix.com/academy and enter code: 171799

31

Verbal Reasoning

CAUSE AND EFFECT

Another regular writing device is **cause and effect**. A cause is an act or event that makes something happen. An effect is what results from the cause. A cause and effect relationship is not always easy to find. So, there are some words and phrases that show causes: *since*, *because*, and *due to*. Words and phrases that show effects include *consequently, therefore, this lead(s) to, as a result*. For example, *Because the sky was clear, Ron did not bring an umbrella*. The cause is the clear sky, and the effect is that Ron did not bring an umbrella. Readers may find that the cause and effect relationship is not clear. For example, *He was late and missed the meeting*. This does not have any words that show cause or effect. Yet, the sentence still has a cause (e.g., he was late) and an effect (e.g., he missed the meeting).

> **Review Video: <u>Rhetorical Strategy of Cause-and-Effect Analysis</u>**
> Visit mometrix.com/academy and enter code: 725944

Remember the chance for a single cause to have many effects. (e.g., *Single cause*: Because you left your homework on the table, your dog eats the homework. *Many effects*: (1) As a result, you fail your homework. (2) Your parents do not let you see your friends. (3) You miss out on the new movie. (4) You miss holding the hand of an important person.)

Also, there is a chance of a single effect to have many causes. (e.g., *Single effect*: Alan has a fever. *Many causes*: (1) An unexpected cold front came through the area, and (2) Alan forgot to take his multi-vitamin.)

Now, an effect can become the cause of another effect. This is known as a cause and effect chain. (e.g., As a result of her hatred for not doing work, Lynn got ready for her exam. This led to her passing her test with high marks. Hence, her resume was accepted, and her application was accepted.)

POINT OF VIEW

The **point of view** of a text is the perspective from which a passage is told. An author will always have a point of view about a story before he or she draws up a plot line. The author will know what events they want to take place, how they want the characters to interact, and how they want the story to resolve. An author will also have an opinion on the topic or series of events which is presented in the story that is based on their prior experience and beliefs.

The two main points of view that authors use--especially in a work of fiction--are first person and third person. If the narrator of the story is also the main character, or *protagonist*, the text is written in first-person point of view. In first person, the author writes from the perspective of *I*. Third-person point of view is probably the most common that authors use in their passages. Using third person, authors refer to each character by using *he* or *she*. In third-person omniscient, the narrator is not a character in the story and tells the story of all of the characters at the same time.

> **Review Video: <u>Point of View</u>**
> Visit mometrix.com/academy and enter code: 383336

TOPICS AND MAIN IDEAS

One of the most important skills in reading comprehension is the identification of **topics** and **main ideas.** There is a subtle difference between these two features. The topic is the **subject** of a text (i.e., what the text is all about). The main idea, on the other hand, is the **most important point** being made by the author. The topic is usually expressed in a few words at the most while the main idea often needs a full sentence to be completely defined. As an example, a short passage might have the topic of penguins and the main idea could be written as *Penguins are different from other birds in many ways*. In most nonfiction writing, the topic and the main idea will be stated directly and often appear in a sentence at the very beginning or end of the text. When being tested on an understanding of the author's topic, you may be able to skim the passage for the general idea, by reading only the first sentence of each paragraph. A body paragraph's first sentence is often—but not always—the main topic sentence which gives you a summary of the content in the paragraph. However, there are cases in which the reader must figure out an unstated topic or main idea. In these instances, you must read every sentence of the text and try to come up with an overarching idea that is supported by each of those sentences.

> **Review Video: Topics and Main Ideas**
> Visit mometrix.com/academy and enter code: 407801

Note: A thesis statement should not be confused with the main idea of the passage. While the main idea gives a brief, general summary of a text, the thesis statement provides a specific perspective on an issue that the author supports with evidence.

SUPPORTING DETAILS

Supporting details provide evidence and backing for the main point. In order to show that a main idea is correct, or valid, authors add details that prove their point. All texts contain details, but they are only classified as supporting details when they serve to reinforce some larger point. Supporting details are most commonly found in informative and persuasive texts. In some cases, they will be clearly indicated with terms like *for example* or *for instance*, or they will be enumerated with terms like *first*, *second*, and *last*. However, you need to be prepared for texts that do not contain those indicators. As a reader, you should consider whether the author's supporting details really back up his or her main point. Supporting details can be factual and correct, yet they may not be relevant to the author's point. Conversely, supporting details can seem pertinent, but they can be ineffective because they are based on opinion or assertions that cannot be proven.

An example of a **main idea** is: *Giraffes live in the Serengeti of Africa*. A **supporting detail** about giraffes could be: *A giraffe in this region benefits from a long neck by reaching twigs and leaves on tall trees.* The main idea expresses that the text is about giraffes in general. The supporting detail gives a specific fact about how the giraffes eat.

> **Review Video: Supporting Details**
> Visit mometrix.com/academy and enter code: 396297

IDENTIFYING THE LOGICAL CONCLUSION

When reading informational texts, there is importance in understanding the logical conclusion of the author's ideas. **Identifying a logical conclusion** can help you determine whether you agree with the writer or not. Coming to this conclusion is much like making an inference: the approach requires you to combine the information given by the text with what you already know in order to make a logical conclusion. If the author intended the reader to draw a certain conclusion, then you can expect the author's argumentation and detail to be leading in that direction. One way to approach the task of drawing conclusions is to make brief notes of all the points made by the author. When the notes are arranged on paper, they may clarify the logical conclusion. Another way to approach conclusions is to consider whether the reasoning of the author raises any pertinent questions. Sometimes you will be able to draw several conclusions from a passage. On occasion

Verbal Reasoning

these will be conclusions that were never imagined by the author. Therefore, be aware that these conclusions must be supported directly by the text.

> **Review Video: How to Support a Conclusion**
> Visit mometrix.com/academy and enter code: 281653

TEXT EVIDENCE

The term **text evidence** refers to information that supports a main point or minor points and can help lead the reader to a conclusion. Information used as text evidence is precise, descriptive, and factual. A main point is often followed by supporting details that provide evidence to back-up a claim. For example, a passage may include the claim that winter occurs during opposite months in the Northern and Southern hemispheres. Text evidence based on this claim may include countries where winter occurs in opposite months along with reasons that winter occurs at different times of the year in separate hemispheres (due to the tilt of the Earth as it rotates around the sun).

> **Review Video: Textual Evidence**
> Visit mometrix.com/academy and enter code: 486236

DIRECTLY STATED INFORMATION

A reader should always be drawing conclusions from the text. Sometimes conclusions are implied from written information, and other times the information is **stated directly** within the passage. One should always aim to draw conclusions from information stated within a passage, rather than to draw them from mere implications.

At times an author may provide some information and then describe a counterargument. Readers should be alert for direct statements that are subsequently rejected or weakened by the author. Furthermore, you should always read through the entire passage before drawing conclusions. Many readers are trained to expect the author's conclusions at either the beginning or the end of the passage, but many texts do not adhere to this format.

IMPLICATIONS

Drawing conclusions from information implied within a passage requires confidence on the part of the reader. **Implications** are things that the author does not state directly, but readers can assume based on what the author does say. Consider the following passage: *I stepped outside and opened my umbrella. By the time I got to work, the cuffs of my pants were soaked*. The author never states that it is raining, but this fact is clearly implied. Conclusions based on implication must be well supported by the text. In order to draw a solid conclusion, readers should have multiple pieces of evidence. If readers have only one piece, they must be assured that there is no other possible explanation than their conclusion. A good reader will be able to draw many conclusions from information implied by the text which will be a great help in the exam.

SUMMARIZING

A helpful tool is the ability to **summarize** the information that you have read in a paragraph or passage format. This process is similar to creating an effective outline. First, a summary should accurately define the main idea of the passage though the summary does not need to explain this main idea in exhaustive detail. The summary should continue by laying out the most important supporting details or arguments from the passage. All of the significant supporting details should be included, and none of the details included should be irrelevant or insignificant. Also, the summary should accurately report all of these details. Too often, the desire for brevity in a summary leads to the sacrifice of clarity or accuracy. Summaries are often difficult to read because they omit all of the

graceful language, digressions, and asides that distinguish great writing. However, an effective summary, it should contain much the same message as the original text.

PARAPHRASING

Paraphrasing is another method that the reader can use to aid in comprehension. When paraphrasing, one puts what they have read into their words by rephrasing what the author has written, or one "translates" all of what the author shared into their words by including as many details as they can.

PREDICTIONS

When reading a good passage, readers are moved to engage actively in the text. One part of being an active reader involves making predictions. A **prediction** is a guess about what will happen next. Readers constantly make predictions based on what they have read and what they already know. Consider the following sentence: *Staring at the computer screen in shock, Kim blindly reached over for the brimming glass of water on the shelf to her side.* The sentence suggests that Kim is agitated, and that she is not looking at the glass that she is going to pick up. So, a reader might predict that Kim is going to knock over the glass. Of course, not every prediction will be accurate: perhaps Kim will pick the glass up cleanly. Nevertheless, the author has certainly created the expectation that the water might be spilled. Predictions are always subject to revision as the reader acquires more information.

INFERENCE

Readers are often required to understand a text that claims and suggests ideas without stating them directly. An **inference** is a piece of information that is implied but not written outright by the author. For instance, consider the following sentence: *After the final out of the inning, the fans were filled with joy and rushed the field.* From this sentence, a reader can infer that the fans were watching a baseball game and their team won the game. Readers should take great care to avoid using information beyond the provided passage before making inferences. As you practice drawing inferences, you will find that they require concentration and attention.

SEQUENCE

Readers must be able to identify a text's **sequence**, or the order in which things happen. Often, when the sequence is very important to the author, the text is indicated with signal words like *first*, *then*, *next*, and *last*. However, a sequence can be merely implied and must be noted by the reader. Consider the sentence *He walked through the garden and gave water and fertilizer to the plants.* Clearly, the man did not walk through the garden before he collected water and fertilizer for the plants, so the implied sequence is that he first collected water, then he collected fertilizer, next he walked through the garden, and last he gave water or fertilizer as necessary to the plants. Texts do not always proceed in an orderly sequence from first to last. Sometimes they begin at the end and

Verbal Reasoning

35

start over at the beginning. As a reader, you can enhance your understanding of the passage by taking brief notes to clarify the sequence.

> **Review Video: <u>Sequence</u>**
> Visit mometrix.com/academy and enter code: 489027

DRAWING CONCLUSIONS

In addition to inference and prediction, readers must often **draw conclusions** about the information they have read. When asked for a *conclusion* that may be drawn, look for critical "hedge" phrases, such as *likely*, *may*, *can*, *will often*, among many others. When you are being tested on this knowledge, remember the question that writers insert into these hedge phrases to cover every possibility. Often an answer will be wrong simply because there is no room for exception. Extreme positive or negative answers (such as always or never) are usually not correct. The reader <u>should not</u> use any outside knowledge that is not gathered from the passage to answer the related questions. Correct answers can be derived straight from the passage.

FACT AND OPINION

Readers must always be conscious of the distinction between fact and opinion. A **fact** can be subjected to analysis and can be either proved or disproved. An **opinion**, on the other hand, is the author's personal thoughts or feelings which may not be alterable by research or evidence. If the author writes that the distance from New York to Boston is about two hundred miles, then he or she is stating a fact. If an author writes that New York is too crowded, then he or she is giving an opinion because there is no objective standard for overpopulation. An opinion may be indicated by words like *believe*, *think*, or *feel*. Readers must be aware that an opinion may be supported by facts. For instance, the author might give the population density of New York as a reason for an overcrowded population. An opinion supported by fact tends to be more convincing. On the other hand, when authors support their opinions with other opinions, readers should not be persuaded by the argument to any degree. When you have an argumentative passage, you need to be sure that facts are presented to the reader from reliable sources. An opinion is what the author thinks about a given topic. An opinion is not common knowledge or proven by expert sources, instead the information is the personal beliefs and thoughts of the author. To distinguish between fact and opinion, a reader needs to consider the type of source that is presenting information, the information that backs-up a claim, and the author's motivation to have a certain point-of-view on a given topic. For example, if a panel of scientists has conducted multiple studies on the effectiveness of taking a certain vitamin, then the results are more likely to be factual than a company that is selling a vitamin and claims that taking the vitamin can produce positive effects. The company is motivated to sell their product, and the scientists are using the scientific method to prove a theory. Remember: if you find sentences that contain phrases such as "I think...", then the statement is an opinion.

> **Review Video: <u>Fact or Opinion</u>**
> Visit mometrix.com/academy and enter code: 870899

BIASES AND STEREOTYPES

In their attempts to persuade, writers often make mistakes in their thinking patterns and writing choices. These patterns and choices are important to understand so you can make an informed decision. Every author has a point-of-view, but authors demonstrate a bias when they ignore reasonable counterarguments or distort opposing viewpoints. A bias is evident whenever the author is unfair or inaccurate in his or her presentation. Bias may be intentional or unintentional, and readers should be skeptical of the author's argument. Remember that a biased author may still

36

be correct; however, the author will be correct in spite of his or her bias, not because of the bias. A **stereotype** is like a bias, yet a stereotype is applied specifically to a group or place. Stereotyping is considered to be particularly abhorrent because the practice promotes negative generalizations about people. Readers should be very cautious of authors who stereotype in their writing. These faulty assumptions typically reveal the author's ignorance and lack of curiosity.

> **Review Video: Bias and Stereotype**
> Visit mometrix.com/academy and enter code: 644829

THE EIGHT PARTS OF SPEECH
NOUNS

When you talk about a person, place, thing, or idea, you are talking about **nouns**. The two main types of nouns are **common** and **proper** nouns. Also, nouns can be abstract (i.e., general) or concrete (i.e., specific).

Common nouns are the class or group of people, places, and things (Note: Do not capitalize common nouns). Examples of common nouns:

People: boy, girl, worker, manager

Places: school, bank, library, home

Things: dog, cat, truck, car

Proper nouns are the names of a specific person, place, or thing (Note: Capitalize all proper nouns). Examples of proper nouns:

People: Abraham Lincoln, George Washington, Martin Luther King, Jr.

Places: Los Angeles, California / New York / Asia

Things: Statue of Liberty, Earth*, Lincoln Memorial

*Note: When you talk about the planet that we live on, you capitalize *Earth*. When you mean the dirt, rocks, or land, you lowercase *earth*.

General nouns are the names of conditions or ideas. **Specific nouns** name people, places, and things that are understood by using your senses.

General nouns:

Condition: beauty, strength

Idea: truth, peace

Specific nouns:

People: baby, friend, father

Places: town, park, city hall

Things: rainbow, cough, apple, silk, gasoline

37

Collective nouns are the names for a person, place, or thing that may act as a whole. The following are examples of collective nouns: *class, company, dozen, group, herd, team,* and *public.*

PRONOUNS

Pronouns are words that are used to stand in for a noun. A pronoun may be classified as personal, intensive, relative, interrogative, demonstrative, indefinite, and reciprocal.

> **Personal:** *Nominative* is the case for nouns and pronouns that are the subject of a sentence. *Objective* is the case for nouns and pronouns that are an object in a sentence. *Possessive* is the case for nouns and pronouns that show possession or ownership.

SINGULAR

	Nominative	Objective	Possessive
First Person	I	me	my, mine
Second Person	you	you	your, yours
Third Person	he, she, it	him, her, it	his, her, hers, its

PLURAL

	Nominative	Objective	Possessive
First Person	we	us	our, ours
Second Person	you	you	your, yours
Third Person	they	them	their, theirs

> **Intensive:** I myself, you yourself, he himself, she herself, the (thing) itself, we ourselves, you yourselves, they themselves
>
> **Relative:** which, who, whom, whose
>
> **Interrogative:** what, which, who, whom, whose
>
> **Demonstrative:** this, that, these, those
>
> **Indefinite:** all, any, each, everyone, either/neither, one, some, several
>
> **Reciprocal:** each other, one another

> **Review Video: Nouns and Pronouns**
> Visit mometrix.com/academy and enter code: 312073

VERBS

If you want to write a sentence, then you need a verb in your sentence. Without a verb, you have no sentence. The verb of a sentence explains action or being. In other words, the verb shows the subject's movement or the movement that has been done to the subject.

TRANSITIVE AND INTRANSITIVE VERBS

A transitive verb is a verb whose action (e.g., drive, run, jump) points to a receiver (e.g., car, dog, kangaroo). Intransitive verbs do not point to a receiver of an action. In other words, the action of the verb does not point to a subject or object.

> **Transitive**: He plays the piano. | The piano was played by him.

> **Intransitive**: He plays. | John writes well.

A dictionary will let you know whether a verb is transitive or intransitive. Some verbs can be transitive and intransitive.

ACTION VERBS AND LINKING VERBS

An action verb is a verb that shows what the subject is doing in a sentence. In other words, an action verb shows action. A sentence can be complete with one word: an action verb. Linking verbs are intransitive verbs that show a condition (i.e., the subject is described but does no action).

Linking verbs link the subject of a sentence to a noun or pronoun, or they link a subject with an adjective. You always need a verb if you want a complete sentence. However, linking verbs are not able to complete a sentence.

Common linking verbs include *appear, be, become, feel, grow, look, seem, smell, sound,* and *taste.* However, any verb that shows a condition and has a noun, pronoun, or adjective that describes the subject of a sentence is a linking verb.

Action: He sings. | Run! | Go! | I talk with him every day. | She reads.

Linking:

> Incorrect: I am.

> Correct: I am John. | I smell roses. | I feel tired.

Note: Some verbs are followed by words that look like prepositions, but they are a part of the verb and a part of the verb's meaning. These are known as phrasal verbs and examples include *call off, look up,* and *drop off.*

> **Review Video: <u>Action Verbs and Linking Verbs</u>**
> Visit mometrix.com/academy and enter code: 743142

VOICE

Transitive verbs come in active or passive voice. If the subject does an action or receives the action of the verb, then you will know whether a verb is active or passive. When the subject of the sentence is doing the action, the verb is **active voice**. When the subject receives the action, the verb is **passive voice**.

> **Active**: Jon drew the picture. (The subject *Jon* is doing the action of *drawing a picture*.)

> **Passive**: The picture is drawn by Jon. (The subject *picture* is receiving the action from Jon.)

VERB TENSES

A verb tense shows the different form of a verb to point to the time of an action. The present and past tense are shown by changing the verb's form. An action in the present *I talk* can change form

Verbal Reasoning

for the past: *I talked*. However, for the other tenses, an auxiliary (i.e., helping) verb is needed to show the change in form. These helping verbs include *am, are, is* | *have, has, had* | *was, were, will* (or *shall*).

Present: I talk	Present perfect: I have talked
Past: I talked	Past perfect: I had talked
Future: I will talk	Future perfect: I will have talked

Present: The action happens at the current time.

> Example: He *walks* to the store every morning.

To show that something is happening right now, use the progressive present tense: I *am walking*.

Past: The action happened in the past.

> Example: He *walked* to the store an hour ago.

Future: The action is going to happen later.

> Example: I *will walk* to the store tomorrow.

Present perfect: The action started in the past and continues into the present.

> Example: I *have walked* to the store three times today.

Past perfect: The second action happened in the past. The first action came before the second.

> Example: Before I walked to the store (Action 2), I *had walked* to the library (Action 1).

Future perfect: An action that uses the past and the future. In other words, the action is complete before a future moment.

> Example: When she comes for the supplies (future moment), I *will have walked* to the store (action completed in the past).

Review Video: <u>Present Perfect, Past Perfect, and Future Perfect Verb Tenses</u>
Visit mometrix.com/academy and enter code: 269472

CONJUGATING VERBS

When you need to change the form of a verb, you are **conjugating** a verb. The key parts of a verb are first person singular, present tense (dream); first person singular, past tense (dreamed); and the past participle (dreamed). Note: the past participle needs a helping verb to make a verb tense. For example, I *have dreamed* of this day. | I *am dreaming* of this day.

Present Tense: Active Voice

	Singular	Plural
First Person	I dream	We dream
Second Person	You dream	You dream
Third Person	He, she, it dreams	They dream

MOOD

There are three moods in English: the indicative, the imperative, and the subjunctive.

The **indicative mood** is used for facts, opinions, and questions.

> Fact: You can do this.
>
> Opinion: I think that you can do this.
>
> Question: Do you know that you can do this?

The **imperative** is used for orders or requests.

> Order: You are going to do this!
>
> Request: Will you do this for me?

The **subjunctive mood** is for wishes and statements that go against fact.

> Wish: I wish that I were going to do this.
>
> Statement against fact: If I were you, I would do this. (This goes against fact because I am not you. You have the chance to do this, and I do not have the chance.)

The mood that causes trouble for most people is the subjunctive mood. If you have trouble with any of the moods, then be sure to practice.

ADJECTIVES

An adjective is a word that is used to modify a noun or pronoun. An adjective answers a question: *Which one? What kind of?* or *How many?* Usually, adjectives come before the words that they modify, but they may also come after a linking verb.

> Which one? The *third* suit is my favorite.
>
> What kind? This suit is *navy blue*.
>
> How many? Can I look over the *four* neckties for the suit?

ARTICLES

Articles are adjectives that are used to mark nouns. There are only three: the **definite** (i.e., limited or fixed amount) article *the*, and the **indefinite** (i.e., no limit or fixed amount) articles *a* and *an*. Note: *An* comes before words that start with a vowel sound (i.e., vowels include *a, e, i, o, u*, and *y*). For example, "Are you going to get an **u**mbrella?"

> **Definite**: I lost *the* bottle that belongs to me.
>
> **Indefinite**: Does anyone have *a* bottle to share?

COMPARISON WITH ADJECTIVES

Some adjectives are relative and other adjectives are absolute. Adjectives that are **relative** can show the comparison between things. Adjectives that are **absolute** can show comparison. However, they show comparison in a different way. Let's say that you are reading two books. You think that one book is perfect, and the other book is not exactly perfect. It is not possible for the book to be

Verbal Reasoning

41

more perfect than the other. Either you think that the book is perfect, or you think that the book is not perfect.

The adjectives that are relative will show the different **degrees** of something or someone to something else or someone else. The three degrees of adjectives include positive, comparative, and superlative.

The **positive** degree is the normal form of an adjective.

Example: This work is *difficult*. | She is *smart*.

The **comparative** degree compares one person or thing to another person or thing.

Example: This work is *more difficult* than your work. | She is *smarter* than me.

The **superlative** degree compares more than two people or things.

Example: This is the *most difficult* work of my life. | She is the *smartest* lady in school.

> **Review Video: Adjectives**
> Visit mometrix.com/academy and enter code: 470154
>
> **Review Video: Comparative and Superlative Adjectives**
> Visit mometrix.com/academy and enter code: 853868

ADVERBS

An adverb is a word that is used to **modify** a verb, adjective, or another adverb. Usually, adverbs answer one of these questions: *When?, Where?, How?,* and *Why?* . The negatives *not* and *never* are known as adverbs. Adverbs that modify adjectives or other adverbs **strengthen** or **weaken** the words that they modify.

Examples:

He walks quickly through the crowd.

The water flows smoothly on the rocks.

Note: While many adverbs end in *-ly*, you need to remember that not all adverbs end in *-ly*. Also, some words that end in *-ly* are adjectives, not adverbs. Some examples include: *early, friendly, holy, lonely, silly*, and *ugly*. To know if a word that ends in *-ly* is an adjective or adverb, you need to check your dictionary.

Examples:

He is *never* angry.

You talk *too* loudly.

COMPARISON WITH ADVERBS

The rules for comparing adverbs are the same as the rules for adjectives.

The **positive** degree is the standard form of an adverb.

Example: He arrives soon. | She speaks softly to her friends.

The **comparative** degree compares one person or thing to another person or thing.

Example: He arrives sooner than Sarah. | She speaks more softly than him.

The **superlative** degree compares more than two people or things.

Example: He arrives soonest of the group. | She speaks most softly of any of her friends.

PREPOSITIONS

A preposition is a word placed before a noun or pronoun that shows the relationship between an object and another word in the sentence.

Common prepositions:

about	before	during	on	under
after	beneath	for	over	until
against	between	from	past	up
among	beyond	in	through	with
around	by	of	to	within
at	down	off	toward	without

Examples:

The napkin is *in* the drawer.

The Earth rotates *around* the Sun.

The needle is *beneath* the haystack.

Can you find me *among* the words?

CONJUNCTIONS

Conjunctions join words, phrases, or clauses, and they show the connection between the joined pieces. **Coordinating** conjunctions connect equal parts of sentences. **Correlative** conjunctions show the connection between pairs. **Subordinating** conjunctions join subordinate (i.e., dependent) clauses with independent clauses.

Verbal Reasoning

COORDINATING CONJUNCTIONS

The coordinating conjunctions include: *and, but, yet, or, nor, for,* and *so*

Examples:

The rock was small, but it was heavy.

She drove in the night, and he drove in the day.

CORRELATIVE CONJUNCTIONS

The correlative conjunctions are: *either...or | neither...nor | not only...but also*

Examples:

Either you are coming *or* you are staying.

He ran *not only* three miles *but also* swam 200 yards.

> **Review Video: Coordinating and Correlative Conjunctions**
> Visit mometrix.com/academy and enter code: 390329

SUBORDINATING CONJUNCTIONS

Common subordinating conjunctions include:

after	since	whenever
although	so that	where
because	unless	wherever
before	until	whether
in order that	when	while

Examples:

I am hungry *because* I did not eat breakfast.

He went home *when* everyone left.

> **Review Video: Subordinating Conjunctions**
> Visit mometrix.com/academy and enter code: 958913

INTERJECTIONS

An interjection is a word for **exclamation** (i.e., great amount of feeling) that is used alone or as a piece to a sentence. Often, they are used at the beginning of a sentence for an **introduction**. Sometimes, they can be used in the middle of a sentence to show a **change** in thought or attitude.

Common Interjections: Hey! | Oh, | Ouch! | Please! | Wow!

Agreement and Sentence Structure

SUBJECTS AND PREDICATES

SUBJECTS

Every sentence has two things: a subject and a verb. The **subject** of a sentence names who or what the sentence is all about. The subject may be directly stated in a sentence, or the subject may be the implied *you*.

The **complete subject** includes the simple subject and all of its modifiers. To find the complete subject, ask *Who* or *What* and insert the verb to complete the question. The answer is the complete subject. To find the **simple subject**, remove all of the modifiers (adjectives, prepositional phrases, etc.) in the complete subject. Being able to locate the subject of a sentence helps with many problems, such as those involving sentence fragments and subject-verb agreement.

Examples:

> The small red car is the one that he wants for Christmas.
>
> (The complete subject is *the small red car.*)
>
> The young artist is coming over for dinner.
>
> (The complete subject is *the young artist.*)

> **Review Video: <u>Subjects in English</u>**
> Visit mometrix.com/academy and enter code: 444771

In **imperative** sentences, the verb's subject is understood (e.g., [You] Run to the store) but not actually present in the sentence. Normally, the subject comes before the verb. However, the subject comes after the verb in sentences that begin with *There are* or *There was*.

Direct:

> John knows the way to the park.
>
> (Who knows the way to the park? Answer: John)
>
> The cookies need ten more minutes.
>
> (What needs ten minutes? Answer: The cookies)
>
> By five o' clock, Bill will need to leave.
>
> (Who needs to leave? Answer: Bill)

Remember: The subject can come after the verb.

> There are five letters on the table for him.
>
> (What is on the table? Answer: Five letters)
>
> There were coffee and doughnuts in the house.
>
> (What was in the house? Answer: Coffee and doughnuts)

45

Verbal Reasoning

Implied:

>Go to the post office for me.

>(Who is going to the post office? Answer: You are.)

>Come and sit with me, please?

>(Who needs to come and sit? Answer: You do.)

PREDICATES

In a sentence, you always have a predicate and a subject. The subject tells what the sentence is about, and the **predicate** explains or describes the subject.

Think about the sentence: *He sings*. In this sentence, we have a subject (He) and a predicate (sings). This is all that is needed for a sentence to be complete. Would we like more information? Of course, we would like to know more. However, if this is all the information that you are given, you have a complete sentence.

Now, let's look at another sentence:

>*John and Jane sing on Tuesday nights at the dance hall.*

What is the subject of this sentence?

>**Answer**: John and Jane.

What is the predicate of this sentence?

>**Answer**: Everything else in the sentence (sing on Tuesday nights at the dance hall).

SUBJECT-VERB AGREEMENT

Verbs **agree** with their subjects in number. In other words, *singular* subjects need *singular* verbs. *Plural* subjects need *plural* verbs. Singular is for one person, place, or thing. Plural is for more than one person, place, or thing. Subjects and verbs must also agree in person: first, second, or third. The present tense ending *-s* is used on a verb if its subject is third person singular; otherwise, the verb takes no ending.

>**Review Video: <u>Subject-Verb Agreement</u>**
>Visit mometrix.com/academy and enter code: 479190

NUMBER AGREEMENT EXAMPLES:

>Single Subject and Verb: *Dan calls home.*

>(Dan is one person. So, the singular verb *calls* is needed.)

>Plural Subject and Verb: *Dan and Bob call home.*

>(More than one person needs the plural verb *call*.)

PERSON AGREEMENT EXAMPLES:

First Person: I *am* walking.

Second Person: You *are* walking.

Third Person: He *is* walking.

COMPLICATIONS WITH SUBJECT-VERB AGREEMENT

WORDS BETWEEN SUBJECT AND VERB

Words that come between the simple subject and the verb may serve as an effective distraction, but they have no bearing on subject-verb agreement.

Examples:

The joy of my life returns home tonight.

(**Singular Subject**: joy. **Singular Verb**: returns)

The phrase *of my life* does not influence the verb *returns*.

The question that still remains unanswered is "Who are you?"

(**Singular Subject**: question. **Singular Verb**: is)

Don't let the phrase "*that still remains…*" trouble you. The subject *question* goes with *is*.

COMPOUND SUBJECTS

A compound subject is formed when two or more nouns joined by *and*, *or*, or *nor* jointly act as the subject of the sentence.

JOINED BY AND

When a compound subject is joined by *and*, it is treated as a plural subject and requires a plural verb.

Examples:

You and Jon are invited to come to my house.

(**Plural Subject**: You and Jon. **Plural Verb**: are)

The pencil and paper belong to me.

(**Plural Subject**: pencil and paper. **Plural Verb**: belong)

JOINED BY OR/NOR

For a compound subject joined by *or* or *nor*, the verb must agree in number with the part of the subject that is closest to the verb (italicized in the examples below).

Examples:

Today or *tomorrow is* the day.

(**Subject**: Today / tomorrow. **Verb**: is)

47

Verbal Reasoning

Stan or *Phil wants* to read the book.

(**Subject**: Stan / Phil. **Verb**: wants)

Neither the books nor the *pen is* on the desk.

(**Subject**: Books / Pen. **Verb**: is)

Either the blanket or *pillows arrive* this afternoon.

(**Subject**: Blanket / Pillows. **Verb**: arrive)

INDEFINITE PRONOUNS AS SUBJECT

An indefinite pronoun is a pronoun that does not refer to a specific noun. Indefinite pronouns may be only singular, be only plural, or change depending on how they are used.

ALWAYS SINGULAR

Pronouns such as *each*, *either*, *everybody*, *anybody*, *somebody*, and *nobody* are always singular.

Examples:

Each of the runners *has* a different bib number.

(**Singular Subject**: Each. **Singular Verb**: has)

Is either of you ready for the game?

(**Singular Subject**: Either. **Singular Verb**: is)

Note: The words *each* and *either* can also be used as adjectives (e.g., *each* person is unique). When one of these adjectives modifies the subject of a sentence, it is always a singular subject.

Everybody grows a day older every day.

(**Singular Subject**: Everybody. **Singular Verb**: grows)

Anybody is welcome to bring a tent.

(**Singular Subject**: Anybody. **Singular Verb**: is)

ALWAYS PLURAL

Pronouns such as *both*, *several*, and *many* are always plural.

Examples:

Both of the siblings *were* too tired to argue.

(**Plural Subject**: Both. **Plural Verb**: were)

Many have tried, but none have succeeded.

(**Plural Subject**: Many. **Plural Verb**: have tried)

DEPEND ON CONTEXT

Pronouns such as *some*, *any*, *all*, *none*, *more*, and *most* can be either singular or plural depending on what they are representing in the context of the sentence.

Examples:

All of my dog's food *was* still there in his bowl

(**Singular Subject**: All. **Singular Verb**: was)

By the end of the night, *all* of my guests *were* already excited about coming to my next party.

(**Plural Subject**: All. **Plural Verb**: were)

OTHER CASES INVOLVING PLURAL OR IRREGULAR FORM

Some nouns are **singular in meaning but plural in form**: news, mathematics, physics, and economics.

The *news is* coming on now.

Mathematics is my favorite class.

Some nouns are plural in form and meaning, and have **no singular equivalent**: scissors and pants.

Do these *pants come* with a shirt?

The *scissors are* for my project.

Mathematical operations are **irregular** in their construction, but are normally considered to be **singular in meaning**.

One plus one is two.

Three times three is nine.

Note: Look to your **dictionary** for help when you aren't sure whether a noun with a plural form has a singular or plural meaning.

COMPLEMENTS

A complement is a noun, pronoun, or adjective that is used to give more information about the subject or verb in the sentence.

DIRECT OBJECTS

A direct object is a noun or pronoun that takes or receives the **action** of a verb. (Remember: a complete sentence does not need a direct object, so not all sentences will have them. A sentence needs only a subject and a verb.) When you are looking for a direct object, find the verb and ask *who* or *what*.

Verbal Reasoning

49

Examples:

> I took the blanket. (Who or what did I take? *The blanket*)
>
> Jane read books. (Who or what does Jane read? *Books*)

INDIRECT OBJECTS

An indirect object is a word or group of words that show how an action had an **influence** on someone or something. If there is an indirect object in a sentence, then you always have a direct object in the sentence. When you are looking for the indirect object, find the verb and ask *to/for whom or what*.

Examples:

> We taught the old dog a new trick.
>
> (To/For Whom or What was taught? *The old dog*)
>
> I gave them a math lesson.
>
> (To/For Whom or What was given? *Them*)

> **Review Video: Direct and Indirect Objects**
> Visit mometrix.com/academy and enter code: 817385

PREDICATE NOMINATIVES AND PREDICATE ADJECTIVES

As we looked at previously, verbs may be classified as either action verbs or linking verbs. A linking verb is so named because it links the subject to words in the predicate that describe or define the subject. These words are called predicate nominatives (if nouns or pronouns) or predicate adjectives (if adjectives).

Examples:

> My father is a *lawyer*.
>
> (Father is the **subject**. Lawyer is the **predicate nominative**.)
>
> Your mother is *patient*.
>
> (Mother is the **subject**. Patient is the **predicate adjective**.)

PRONOUN USAGE

The **antecedent** is the noun that has been replaced by a pronoun. A pronoun and its antecedent **agree** when they have the same number (singular or plural) and gender (male, female, or neuter).

Examples:

> **Singular agreement**: *John* came into town, and *he* played for us.
>
> (The word *he* replaces *John*.)
>
> **Plural agreement**: *John and Rick* came into town, and *they* played for us.
>
> (The word *they* replaces *John and Rick*.)

To determine which is the correct pronoun to use in a compound subject or object, try each pronoun **alone** in place of the compound in the sentence. Your knowledge of pronouns will tell you which one is correct.

Example:

Bob and (I, me) will be going.

Test: (1) *I will be going* or (2) *Me will be going.* The second choice cannot be correct because *me* cannot be used as the subject of a sentence. Instead, *me* is used as an object.

Answer: Bob and I will be going.

When a pronoun is used with a noun immediately following (as in "we boys"), try the sentence **without the added noun**.

Example:

(We/Us) boys played football last year.

Test: (1) *We played football last ye*ar or (2) *Us played football last year*. Again, the second choice cannot be correct because *us* cannot be used as a subject of a sentence. Instead, *us* is used as an object.

Answer: We boys played football last year.

Review Video: <u>Pronoun Usage</u>
Visit mometrix.com/academy and enter code: 666500

Review Video: <u>Pronoun-Antecedent Agreement</u>
Visit mometrix.com/academy and enter code: 919704

A pronoun should point clearly to the **antecedent**. Here is how a pronoun reference can be unhelpful if it is not directly stated or puzzling.

Unhelpful: Ron and Jim went to the store, and *he* bought soda.

(Who bought soda? Ron or Jim?)

Helpful: Jim went to the store, and *he* bought soda.

(The sentence is clear. Jim bought the soda.)

Some pronouns change their form by their placement in a sentence. A pronoun that is a subject in a sentence comes in the **subjective case**. Pronouns that serve as objects appear in the **objective case**. Finally, the pronouns that are used as possessives appear in the **possessive case**.

Examples:

Subjective case: *He* is coming to the show.

(The pronoun *He* is the subject of the sentence.)

Verbal Reasoning

51

Objective case: Josh drove *him* to the airport.

(The pronoun *him* is the object of the sentence.)

Possessive case: The flowers are *mine*.

(The pronoun *mine* shows ownership of the flowers.)

The word *who* is a subjective-case pronoun that can be used as a **subject**. The word *whom* is an objective-case pronoun that can be used as an **object**. The words *who* and *whom* are common in subordinate clauses or in questions.

Examples:

Subject: He knows who wants to come.

(*Who* is the subject of the verb *wants*.)

Object: He knows the man whom we want at the party.

(*Whom* is the object of *we want*.)

CLAUSES

A clause is a group of words that contains both a subject and a predicate (verb). There are two types of clauses: independent and dependent. An **independent clause** contains a complete thought, while a **dependent (or subordinate) clause** does not. A dependent clause includes a subject and a verb, and may also contain objects or complements, but it cannot stand as a complete thought without being joined to an independent clause. Dependent clauses function within sentences as adjectives, adverbs, or nouns.

Example:

Independent Clause: I am running

Dependent Clause: because I want to stay in shape

The clause *I am running* is an independent clause: it has a subject and a verb, and it gives a complete thought. The clause *because I want to stay in shape* is a dependent clause: it has a subject and a verb, but it does not express a complete thought. It adds detail to the independent clause to which it is attached.

Combined: I am running because I want to stay in shape.

> **Review Video: Clauses**
> Visit mometrix.com/academy and enter code: 940170
>
> **Review Video: Independent and Dependent Clause Examples**
> Visit mometrix.com/academy and enter code: 556903

Types of Dependent Clauses
Adjective Clauses

An **adjective clause** is a dependent clause that modifies a noun or a pronoun. Adjective clauses begin with a relative pronoun (*who, whose, whom, which,* and *that*) or a relative adverb (*where, when,* and *why*).

Also, adjective clauses come after the noun that the clause needs to explain or rename. This is done to have a clear connection to the independent clause.

Examples:

I learned the reason *why I won the award*.

This is the place *where I started my first job*.

An adjective clause can be an essential or nonessential clause. An essential clause is very important to the sentence. **Essential clauses** explain or define a person or thing. **Nonessential clauses** give more information about a person or thing but are not necessary to define them. Nonessential clauses are set off with commas while essential clauses are not.

Examples:

Essential: A person *who works hard at first* can often rest later in life.

Nonessential: Neil Armstrong, *who walked on the moon*, is my hero.

> **Review Video: Adjective Clauses and Phrases**
> Visit mometrix.com/academy and enter code: 520888

Adverb Clauses

An **adverb clause** is a dependent clause that modifies a verb, adjective, or adverb. In sentences with multiple dependent clauses, adverb clauses are usually placed immediately before or after the independent clause. An adverb clause is introduced with words such as *after, although, as, before, because, if, since, so, unless, when, where*, and *while*.

Examples:

When you walked outside, I called the manager.

I will go with you *unless you want to stay*.

Noun Clauses

A **noun clause** is a dependent clause that can be used as a subject, object, or complement. Noun clauses begin with words such as *how, that, what, whether, which, who,* and *why*. These words can also come with an adjective clause. Unless the noun clause is being used as the subject of the sentence, it should come after the verb of the independent clause.

Examples:

The real mystery is *how you avoided serious injury*.

What you learn from each other depends on your honesty with others.

53

SUBORDINATION

When two related ideas are not of equal importance, the ideal way to combine them is to make the more important idea an independent clause, and the less important idea a dependent or subordinate clause. This is called **subordination**.

Example:

> **Separate ideas**: The team had a perfect regular season. The team lost the championship.

> **Subordinated**: Despite having a perfect regular season, *the team lost the championship.*

PHRASES

A phrase is a group of words that functions as a single part of speech, usually a noun, adjective, or adverb. A phrase is not a complete thought, but it adds **detail** or **explanation** to a sentence, or **renames** something within the sentence.

PREPOSITIONAL PHRASES

One of the most common types of phrases is the prepositional phrase. A **prepositional phrase** begins with a preposition and ends with a noun or pronoun that is the object of the preposition. Normally, the prepositional phrase functions as an **adjective** or an **adverb** within the sentence.

Examples:

> The picnic is *on the blanket.*

> I am sick *with a fever* today.

> *Among the many flowers*, John found a four-leaf clover.

VERBAL PHRASES

A verbal is a word or phrase that is formed from a verb but does not function as a verb. Depending on its particular form, it may be used as a noun, adjective, or adverb. A verbal does **not** replace a verb in a sentence.

Examples:

> Correct: *Walk* a mile daily.

> (*Walk* is the verb of this sentence. The subject is the implied *you*.)

> Incorrect: *To walk* a mile.

> (*To walk* is a type of verbal. This is not a sentence since there is no functional verb)

There are three types of verbals: **participles**, **gerunds**, and **infinitives**. Each type of verbal has a corresponding **phrase** that consists of the verbal itself along with any complements or modifiers.

PARTICIPLES

A **participle** is a type of verbal that always functions as an adjective. The present participle always ends with *-ing*. Past participles end with *-d, -ed, -n,* or *-t.*

> Examples: Verb: *dance* | Present Participle: *dancing* | Past Participle: *danced*

Participial phrases most often come right before or right after the noun or pronoun that they modify.

Examples:

Shipwrecked on an island, the boys started to fish for food.

Having been seated for five hours, we got out of the car to stretch our legs.

Praised for their work, the group accepted the first-place trophy.

GERUNDS

A **gerund** is a type of verbal that always functions as a noun. Like present participles, gerunds always end with *-ing*, but they can be easily distinguished from one another by the part of speech they represent (participles always function as adjectives). Since a gerund or gerund phrase always functions as a noun, it can be used as the subject of a sentence, the predicate nominative, or the object of a verb or preposition.

Examples:

We want to be known for *teaching the poor*. (Object of preposition)

Coaching this team is the best job of my life. (Subject)

We like *practicing our songs* in the basement. (Object of verb)

INFINITIVES

An **infinitive** is a type of verbal that can function as a noun, an adjective, or an adverb. An infinitive is made of the word *to* + the basic form of the verb. As with all other types of verbal phrases, an infinitive phrase includes the verbal itself and all of its complements or modifiers.

Examples:

To join the team is my goal in life. (Noun)

The animals have enough food *to eat for the night*. (Adjective)

People lift weights *to exercise their muscles*. (Adverb)

> **Review Video: Gerunds, Participles, and Infinitives**
> Visit mometrix.com/academy and enter code: 634263

APPOSITIVE PHRASES

An **appositive** is a word or phrase that is used to explain or rename nouns or pronouns. Noun phrases, gerund phrases, and infinitive phrases can all be used as appositives.

Verbal Reasoning

55

Examples:

> Terriers, *hunters at heart*, have been dressed up to look like lap dogs.

> (The noun phrase *hunters at heart* renames the noun *terriers*.)

> His plan, *to save and invest his money*, was proven as a safe approach.

> (The infinitive phrase explains what the plan is.)

Appositive phrases can be **essential** or **nonessential**. An appositive phrase is essential if the person, place, or thing being described or renamed is too general for its meaning to be understood without the appositive.

Examples:

> **Essential**: Two Founding Fathers George Washington and Thomas Jefferson served as presidents.

> **Nonessential**: George Washington and Thomas Jefferson, two Founding Fathers, served as presidents.

Absolute Phrases

An absolute phrase is a phrase that consists of **a noun followed by a participle**. An absolute phrase provides **context** to what is being described in the sentence, but it does not modify or explain any particular word; it is essentially independent.

Examples:

> *The alarm ringing*, he pushed the snooze button.

> *The music paused*, she continued to dance through the crowd.

Note: Absolute phrases can be confusing, so don't be discouraged if you have a difficult time with them.

Parallelism

When multiple items or ideas are presented in a sentence in series, such as in a list, the items or ideas must be stated in grammatically equivalent ways. In other words, if one idea is stated in gerund form, the second cannot be stated in infinitive form. For example, to write, *I enjoy reading and to study* would be incorrect. An infinitive and a gerund are not equivalent. Instead, you should write *I enjoy reading and studying*. In lists of more than two, it can be harder to keep everything straight, but all items in a list must be parallel.

Example:

> **Incorrect**: He stopped at the office, grocery store, and the pharmacy before heading home.

> The first and third items in the list of places include the article *the*, so the second item needs it as well.

> **Correct**: He stopped at the office, *the* grocery store, and the pharmacy before heading home.

56

Example:

Incorrect: While vacationing in Europe, she went biking, skiing, and climbed mountains.

The first and second items in the list are gerunds, so the third item must be as well.

Correct: While vacationing in Europe, she went biking, skiing, and *mountain climbing*.

> **Review Video: Parallel Sentence Construction**
> Visit mometrix.com/academy and enter code: 831988

SENTENCE PURPOSE

There are four types of sentences: declarative, imperative, interrogative, and exclamatory.

A **declarative** sentence states a fact and ends with a period.

Example: *The football game starts at seven o'clock.*

An **imperative** sentence tells someone to do something and generally ends with a period. (An urgent command might end with an exclamation point instead.)

Example: *Don't forget to buy your ticket.*

An **interrogative** sentence asks a question and ends with a question mark.

Example: *Are you going to the game on Friday?*

An **exclamatory** sentence shows strong emotion and ends with an exclamation point.

Example: *I can't believe we won the game!*

SENTENCE STRUCTURE

Sentences are classified by structure based on the type and number of clauses present. The four classifications of sentence structure are the following:

Simple: A simple sentence has one independent clause with no dependent clauses. A simple sentence may have **compound elements** (i.e., compound subject or verb).

Examples:

Judy *watered* the lawn. (single <u>subject</u>, single *verb*)

Judy and Alan *watered* the lawn. (compound <u>subject</u>, single *verb*)

Judy *watered* the lawn and *pulled* weeds. (single <u>subject</u>, compound *verb*)

Judy and Alan *watered* the lawn and *pulled* weeds. (compound <u>subject</u>, compound *verb*)

Compound: A compound sentence has two or more <u>independent clauses</u> with no dependent clauses. Usually, the independent clauses are joined with a comma and a coordinating conjunction or with a semicolon.

Verbal Reasoning

Examples:

    <u>The time has come</u>, and <u>we are ready</u>.

    <u>I woke up at dawn</u>; <u>the sun was just coming up</u>.

Complex: A complex sentence has one <u>independent clause</u> and at least one *dependent clause*.

Examples:

    Although he had the flu, <u>Harry went to work</u>.

    <u>Marcia got married</u> *after she finished college*.

Compound-Complex: A compound-complex sentence has at least two <u>independent clauses</u> and at least one *dependent clause*.

    Examples:

    <u>John is my friend</u> *who went to India*, and <u>he brought back souvenirs</u>.

    <u>You may not realize this</u>, but <u>we heard the music</u> *that you played last night*.

Review Video: <u>Sentence Structure</u>
Visit mometrix.com/academy and enter code: 700478

Review Video: <u>Intro to Sentence Types</u>
Visit mometrix.com/academy and enter code: 953367

SENTENCE FRAGMENTS

Usually when the term *sentence fragment* comes up, it is because you have to decide whether or not a group of words is a complete sentence, and if it's not a complete sentence, you're about to have to fix it. Recall that a group of words must contain at least one **independent clause** in order to be considered a sentence. If it doesn't contain even one independent clause, it would be called a **sentence fragment**. (If it contains two or more independent clauses that are not joined correctly, it would be called a run-on sentence.)

The process to use for **repairing** a sentence fragment depends on what type of fragment it is. If the fragment is a dependent clause, it can sometimes be as simple as removing a subordinating word (e.g., when, because, if) from the beginning of the fragment. Alternatively, a dependent clause can be incorporated into a closely related neighboring sentence. If the fragment is missing some required part, like a subject or a verb, the fix might be as simple as adding it in.

Examples:

    Fragment: Because he wanted to sail the Mediterranean.

    Removed subordinating word: He wanted to sail the Mediterranean.

    Combined with another sentence: Because he wanted to sail the Mediterranean, he booked a Greek island cruise.

58

RUN-ON SENTENCES

Run-on sentences consist of multiple independent clauses that have not been joined together properly. Run-on sentences can be corrected in several different ways:

Join clauses properly: This can be done with a comma and coordinating conjunction, with a semicolon, or with a colon or dash if the second clause is explaining something in the first.

Example:

>   **Incorrect**: I went on the trip, we visited lots of castles.

>   **Corrected**: I went on the trip, and we visited lots of castles.

Split into separate sentences: This correction is most effective when the independent clauses are very long or when they are not closely related.

Example:

>   **Incorrect**: The drive to New York takes ten hours, my uncle lives in Boston.

>   **Corrected**: The drive to New York takes ten hours. My uncle lives in Boston.

Make one clause dependent: This is the easiest way to make the sentence correct and more interesting at the same time. It's often as simple as adding a subordinating word between the two clauses

Example:

>   **Incorrect**: I finally made it to the store and I bought some eggs.

>   **Corrected**: When I finally made it to the store, I bought some eggs.

Reduce to one clause with a compound verb: If both clauses have the same subject, remove the subject from the second clause, and you now have just one clause with a compound verb.

Example:

>   **Incorrect**: The drive to New York takes ten hours, it makes me very tired.

>   **Corrected**: The drive to New York takes ten hours and makes me very tired.

Note: While these are the simplest ways to correct a run-on sentence, often the best way is to completely reorganize the thoughts in the sentence and rewrite it.

> **Review Video: <u>Fragments and Run-on Sentences</u>**
> Visit mometrix.com/academy and enter code: 541989

DANGLING AND MISPLACED MODIFIERS

DANGLING MODIFIERS

A dangling modifier is a dependent clause or verbal phrase that does not have a **clear logical connection** to a word in the sentence.

Example:

Dangling: *Reading each magazine article*, the stories caught my attention.

The word *stories* cannot be modified by *Reading each magazine article*. People can read, but stories cannot read. Therefore, the subject of the sentence must be a person.

Corrected: Reading each magazine article, *I* was entertained by the stories.

Example:

Dangling: Ever since childhood, my grandparents have visited me for Christmas.

The speaker in this sentence can't have been visited by her grandparents when *they* were children, since she wouldn't have been born yet. Either the modifier should be **clarified** or the sentence should be **rearranged** to specify whose childhood is being referenced.

Clarified: Ever since I was a child, my grandparents have visited for Christmas.

Rearranged: Ever since childhood, I have enjoyed my grandparents visiting for Christmas.

MISPLACED MODIFIERS

Because modifiers are grammatically versatile, they can be put in many different places within the structure of a sentence. The danger of this versatility is that a modifier can accidentally be placed where it is modifying the wrong word or where it is not clear which word it is modifying.

Example:

Misplaced: She read the book to a crowd *that was filled with beautiful pictures*.

The book was filled with beautiful pictures, not the crowd.

Corrected: She read the book *that was filled with beautiful pictures* to a crowd.

Example:

Ambiguous: Derek saw a bus nearly hit a man *on his way to work*.

Was Derek on his way to work? Or was the other man?

Derek: *On his way to work*, Derek saw a bus nearly hit a man.

The other man: Derek saw a bus nearly hit a man *who was on his way to work*.

SPLIT INFINITIVES

A split infinitive occurs when a modifying word comes between the word *to* and the verb that pairs with *to*.

Example: To *clearly* explain vs. *To explain* clearly | To *softly* sing vs. *To sing* softly

Though considered improper by some, split infinitives may provide better clarity and simplicity in some cases than the alternatives. As such, avoiding them should not be considered a universal rule.

DOUBLE NEGATIVES

Standard English allows **two negatives** only when a **positive** meaning is intended. For example, *The team was not displeased with their performance.* Double negatives to emphasize negation are not used in standard English.

Negative modifiers (e.g., never, no, and not) should not be paired with other negative modifiers or negative words (e.g., none, nobody, nothing, or neither). The modifiers *hardly, barely*, and *scarcely* are considered negatives in standard English, so they should not be used with other negatives.

Punctuation

END PUNCTUATION

PERIODS

Use a period to end all sentences except direct questions, exclamations.

DECLARATIVE SENTENCE

A declarative sentence gives information or makes a statement.

Examples: I can fly a kite. | The plane left two hours ago.

IMPERATIVE SENTENCE

An imperative sentence gives an order or command.

Examples: You are coming with me. | Bring me that note.

PERIODS FOR ABBREVIATIONS

Examples: 3 P.M. | 2 A.M. | Mr. Jones | Mrs. Stevens | Dr. Smith | Bill Jr. | Pennsylvania Ave.

Note: an abbreviation is a shortened form of a word or phrase.

QUESTION MARKS

Question marks should be used following a direct question. A polite request can be followed by a period instead of a question mark.

Direct Question: What is for lunch today? | How are you? | Why is that the answer?

Polite Requests: Can you please send me the item tomorrow. | Will you please walk with me on the track.

> **Review Video: When to Use a Question Mark**
> Visit mometrix.com/academy and enter code: 118471

EXCLAMATION MARKS

Exclamation marks are used after a word group or sentence that shows much feeling or has special importance. Exclamation marks should not be overused. They are saved for proper **exclamatory interjections**.

Example: We're going to the finals! | You have a beautiful car! | That's crazy!

> **Review Video: What Does an Exclamation Point Mean?**
> Visit mometrix.com/academy and enter code: 199367

COMMAS

The comma is a punctuation mark that can help you understand connections in a sentence. Not every sentence needs a comma. However, if a sentence needs a comma, you need to put it in the right place. A comma in the wrong place (or an absent comma) will make a sentence's meaning unclear. These are some of the rules for commas:

1. Use a comma **before a coordinating conjunction** joining independent clauses
   Example: Bob caught three fish, and I caught two fish.

62

2. Use a comma after an introductory phrase or an adverbial clause

   Examples:

   > *After the final out,* we went to a restaurant to celebrate.
   > *Studying the stars,* I was surprised at the beauty of the sky.

3. Use a comma between items in a series.

   Example: I will bring the turkey, the pie, and the coffee.

4. Use a comma **between coordinate adjectives** not joined with *and*

   Incorrect: The kind, brown dog followed me home.
   Correct: The *kind, loyal* dog followed me home.
   Not all adjectives are **coordinate** (i.e., equal or parallel). There are two simple ways to know if your adjectives are coordinate. One, you can join the adjectives with *and*: *The kind and loyal dog.* Two, you can change the order of the adjectives: *The loyal, kind dog.*

5. Use commas for **interjections** and **after** *yes* and *no* responses

   Examples:

   > **Interjection**: Oh, I had no idea. | Wow, you know how to play this game.
   > **Yes and No**: *Yes,* I heard you. | *No,* I cannot come tomorrow.

6. Use commas to separate nonessential modifiers and nonessential appositives

   Examples:

   > **Nonessential Modifier**: John Frank, who is coaching the team, was promoted today.
   > **Nonessential Appositive**: Thomas Edison, an American inventor, was born in Ohio.

7. Use commas to set off nouns of direct address, interrogative tags, and contrast

   Examples:

   > **Direct Address**: You, *John,* are my only hope in this moment.
   > **Interrogative Tag**: This is the last time, *correct*?
   > **Contrast**: You are my friend, *not my enemy.*

8. Use commas with dates, addresses, geographical names, and titles

   Examples:

   > **Date**: *July 4, 1776,* is an important date to remember.
   > **Address**: He is meeting me at *456 Delaware Avenue, Washington, D.C.,* tomorrow morning.
   > **Geographical Name**: *Paris, France,* is my favorite city.
   > **Title**: John Smith, *Ph. D.,* will be visiting your class today.

9. Use commas to **separate expressions like *he said*** and ***she said*** if they come between a sentence of a quote

   Examples:

   > "I want you to know," he began, "that I always wanted the best for you."
   > "You can start," Jane said, "with an apology."

Review Video: <u>When To Use a Comma</u>
Visit mometrix.com/academy and enter code: 786797

63

SEMICOLONS

The semicolon is used to connect major sentence pieces of equal value. Some rules for semicolons include:

1. Use a semicolon **between closely connected independent clauses** that are not connected with a coordinating conjunction.

   Examples:

   > She is outside; we are inside.
   > You are right; we should go with your plan.

2. Use a semicolon **between independent clauses linked with a transitional word.**

   Examples:

   > I think that we can agree on this; *however,* I am not sure about my friends.
   > You are looking in the wrong places; *therefore,* you will not find what you need.

3. Use a semicolon **between items in a series that has internal punctuation.**

   Example: I have visited New York, New York; Augusta, Maine; and Baltimore, Maryland.

> **Review Video: How to Use Semicolons**
> Visit mometrix.com/academy and enter code: 370605

COLONS

The colon is used to call attention to the words that follow it. A colon must come after a **complete independent clause**. The rules for colons are as follows:

1. Use a colon after an independent clause to **make a list**

   Example: I want to learn many languages: Spanish, German, and Italian.

2. Use a colon for **explanations** or to **give a quote**

   Examples:

   > **Quote**: He started with an idea: "We are able to do more than we imagine."
   > **Explanation**: There is one thing that stands out on your resume: responsibility.

3. Use a colon **after the greeting in a formal letter**, to **show hours and minutes**, and to **separate a title and subtitle**

   Examples:

   > **Greeting in a formal letter**: Dear Sir: | To Whom It May Concern:
   > **Time**: It is 3:14 P.M.
   > **Title**: The essay is titled "America: A Short Introduction to a Modern Country"

> **Review Video: What is a Colon?**
> Visit mometrix.com/academy and enter code: 868673

PARENTHESES

Parentheses are used for additional information. Also, they can be used to put labels for letters or numbers in a series. Parentheses should be not be used very often. If they are overused, parentheses can be a distraction instead of a help.

Examples:

Extra Information: The rattlesnake (see Image 2) is a dangerous snake of North and South America.

Series: Include in the email (1) your name, (2) your address, and (3) your question for the author.

> **Review Video: When to Use Parentheses**
> Visit mometrix.com/academy and enter code: 947743

QUOTATION MARKS

Use quotation marks to close off **direct quotations** of a person's spoken or written words. Do not use quotation marks around indirect quotations. An indirect quotation gives someone's message without using the person's exact words. Use **single quotation marks** to close off a quotation inside a quotation.

Direct Quote: Nancy said, "I am waiting for Henry to arrive."

Indirect Quote: Henry said that he is going to be late to the meeting.

Quote inside a Quote: The teacher asked, "Has everyone read 'The Gift of the Magi'?"

Quotation marks should be used around the titles of **short works**: newspaper and magazine articles, poems, short stories, songs, television episodes, radio programs, and subdivisions of books or web sites.

Examples:

"Rip van Winkle" (short story by Washington Irving)

"O Captain! My Captain!" (poem by Walt Whitman)

Although it is not standard usage, quotation marks are sometimes used to highlight **irony**, or the use of words to mean something other than their dictionary definition. This type of usage should be employed sparingly, if at all.

Examples:

The boss warned Frank that he was walking on "thin ice."

(Frank is not walking on real ice. Instead, Frank is being warned to avoid mistakes.)

The teacher thanked the young man for his "honesty."

(In this example, the quotation marks around *honesty* show that the teacher does not believe the young man's explanation.)

> **Review Video: Quotation Marks**
> Visit mometrix.com/academy and enter code: 884918

Periods and commas are put **inside** quotation marks. Colons and semicolons are put **outside** the quotation marks. Question marks and exclamation points are placed inside quotation marks when

Verbal Reasoning

they are part of a quote. When the question or exclamation mark goes with the whole sentence, the mark is left outside of the quotation marks.

Examples:

Period and comma: We read "The Gift of the Magi," "The Skylight Room," and "The Cactus."

Semicolon: They watched "The Nutcracker"; then, they went home.

Exclamation mark that is a part of a quote: The crowd cheered, "Victory!"

Question mark that goes with the whole sentence: Is your favorite short story "The Tell-Tale Heart"?

APOSTROPHES

An apostrophe is used to show **possession** or the **deletion of letters in contractions**. An apostrophe is not needed with the possessive pronouns *his, hers, its, ours, theirs, whose*, and *yours*.

Singular Nouns: David's car | a book's theme | my brother's board game

Plural Nouns with -s: the scissors' handle | boys' basketball

Plural Nouns without -s: Men's department | the people's adventure

> **Review Video: When to Use an Apostrophe**
> Visit mometrix.com/academy and enter code: 213068
>
> **Review Video: Punctuation Errors in Possessive Pronouns**
> Visit mometrix.com/academy and enter code: 221438

HYPHENS

Hyphens are used to **separate compound words**. Use hyphens in the following cases:

1. **Compound numbers** between 21 and 99 when written out in words
   Example: This team needs *twenty-five* points to win the game.

2. **Written-out fractions** that are used as **adjectives**
   Correct: The recipe says that we need a *three-fourths* cup of butter.
   Incorrect: *One-fourth* of the road is under construction.

3. Compound words used as **adjectives that come before a noun**
   Correct: The *well-fed* dog took a nap.
   Incorrect: The dog was *well-fed* for his nap.

4. Compound words that would be **hard to read** or **easily confused with other words**
   Examples: Semi-irresponsible | Anti-itch | Re-sort

Note: This is not a complete set of the rules for hyphens. A dictionary is the best tool for knowing if a compound word needs a hyphen.

> **Review Video: Hyphens**
> Visit mometrix.com/academy and enter code: 981632

DASHES

Dashes are used to show a **break** or a **change in thought** in a sentence or to act as parentheses in a sentence. When typing, use two hyphens to make a dash. Do not put a space before or after the dash. The following are the rules for dashes:

1. To set off **parenthetical statements** or an **appositive with internal punctuation**

   Example: The three trees—oak, pine, and magnolia—are coming on a truck tomorrow.

2. To show a **break or change in tone or thought**

   Example: The first question—how silly of me—does not have a correct answer.

ELLIPSIS MARKS

The ellipsis mark has three periods (…) to show when **words have been removed** from a quotation. If a full sentence or more is removed from a quoted passage, you need to use four periods to show the removed text and the end punctuation mark. The ellipsis mark should not be used at the beginning of a quotation. The ellipsis mark should also not be used at the end of a quotation unless some words have been deleted from the end of the final sentence.

Example:

"Then he picked up the groceries…paid for them…later he went home."

BRACKETS

There are two main reasons to use brackets:

1. When **placing parentheses inside of parentheses**

   Example: The hero of this story, Paul Revere (a silversmith and industrialist [see Ch. 4]), rode through towns of Massachusetts to warn of advancing British troops.

2. When adding **clarification or detail** to a quotation that is **not part of the quotation**
   Example:

   The father explained, "My children are planning to attend my alma mater [State University]."

Review Video: <u>Using Brackets in Sentences</u>
Visit mometrix.com/academy and enter code: 727546

Review Video: <u>The Importance of Consistency in Punctuation</u>
Visit mometrix.com/academy and enter code: 169489

Verbal Reasoning

67

Data Insights

LOGICAL ORGANIZATION

There are six major types of logical organization that are frequently used:

1. Illustrations may be used to support the thesis. Examples are the most common form of this organization.
2. A series of definitions identifying what something is or is not is another way of organization. What are the characteristics of the topic?
3. Dividing or classifying information into separate items according to their similarities is a common and effective organizing method.
4. Comparing, focusing on the similarities of things, and contrasting, highlighting the differences between things, together form an excellent tool to use with certain kinds of information.
5. Cause and effect is a simple tool to logically understand relationships between things. A phenomenon may be traced to its causes for organizing a subject logically.
6. Problem and solution is a simple and effective manner of logically organizing material. It is very commonly used and lucidly presents information.

PRODUCING CLEAR AND COHERENT WRITING APPROPRIATE TO THE TASK, PURPOSE, AND AUDIENCE

Each genre of writing requires its own traits, but to attain clear and coherent writing it is necessary to plan what you will be writing. First, decide on your goal, or whether you are trying to inform, persuade, or entertain. With your goal in mind, you need to organize your material if you are writing a nonfiction piece. You need to have a clear idea of your main ideas and supporting details. If you are planning to write a narrative, you need to pay attention to developing your story in a clear and flowing manner. Then, create characters through skillful use of description, dialogue, and action. In addition, in all types of writing you need to establish a tone. You also need to make sure your writing is free of grammatical or spelling errors. Close rereading and editing is part of the writing process, as well.

ANALYSIS OF RELATIONSHIPS BETWEEN SIMILAR IDEAS AND IDEAS IN OPPOSITION

Many texts follow the **compare-and-contrast** model in which the similarities and differences between two ideas or things are explored. Analysis of the similarities between ideas is called comparison. In an ideal comparison, the author places ideas or things in an equivalent structure (i.e., the author presents the ideas in the same way). If an author wants to show the similarities between cricket and baseball, then he or she may do so by summarizing the equipment and rules for each game. Be mindful of the similarities as they appear in the passage and take note of any differences that are mentioned. Often, these small differences will only reinforce the more general similarity.

Thinking critically about ideas and conclusions can seem like a daunting task. One way to ease this task is to understand the basic elements of ideas and writing techniques. Looking at the way different ideas relate to each other can be a good way for readers to begin their analysis. For instance, sometimes authors will write about two ideas that are in opposition to each other. Or one author will provide his or her ideas on a topic, and another author may respond in opposition. The analysis of these opposing ideas is known as **contrast**. Contrast is often marred by the author's obvious partiality to one of the ideas. A discerning reader will be put off by an author who does not engage in a fair fight.

In an analysis of opposing ideas, both ideas should be presented in clear and reasonable terms. If the author does prefer a side, you need to read carefully to determine the areas where the author shows or avoids this preference. In an analysis of opposing ideas, you should proceed through the passage by marking the major differences point by point with an eye that is looking for an explanation of each side's view. For instance, in an analysis of capitalism and communism, there is an importance in outlining each side's view on labor, markets, prices, personal responsibility, etc. Additionally, as you read through the passages, you should note whether the opposing views present each side in a similar manner.

> **Review Video: Compare and Contrast**
> Visit mometrix.com/academy and enter code: 798319

TABLES AND GRAPHS

Tables present information that has been observed in a field of study and has been collected into a visual format for ease of reading and understanding. At the top of the table, there will be a title which consists of a short phrase indicating the information that the table or graph intends to convey. The title of a table could be something like *Average Income for Various Education Levels* or *Price of Milk Compared to Demand*. A table is composed of information laid out in vertical columns and horizontal rows. Typically, each column will have a label. If *Average Income for Various Education Levels* was placed in a table format, then the two columns could be labeled *Education Level* and *Average Income*. Each location on the table is called a cell. Cells are defined by their column and row (e.g., second column, fifth row). The obtained information for a table is placed within these cells.

BAR GRAPH AND LINE GRAPH

Readers need to consider the intention and the structure of a graph format. For instance, a **bar graph** is appropriate for displaying distinct quantities on a scale and showing the variation among those quantities. If one wanted to display the amount of money spent on groceries during the months of a year, then a bar graph would be appropriate. The vertical axis would represent values of money, and the horizontal axis would identify the bar representing each month. On the other hand, if the grocery expenses were plotted on a line graph instead of a bar graph, there would be an emphasis on whether the amount of spending rose or fell over the course of the year.

Whereas a bar graph is good for showing the relationships between the different values plotted, the **line graph** is good for showing whether the values tend to increase, decrease, or remain stable. Generally, the bar graph is preferable to the line graph since there has to be some built-in relationship between the data points because the graph implies a relationship (e.g., the amount of different apples at a store or the speed of popular rollercoasters at an amusement park). The line graph is superior in particular situations (e.g., intervals of time or development) because the line graph shows the rate of change between period of times in a visual format (e.g., observing a stock on the Dow Jones rise and fall over the course of a month or tracking the height of a child over a period of years).

> **Review Video: How to Create a Line Graph**
> Visit mometrix.com/academy and enter code: 480147

Data Insights

PIE CHART

A **pie chart**, also known as a circle graph, is useful for depicting how a single unit or category is divided. The standard pie chart is a circle with designated wedges. Each wedge is proportional in size to a part of the whole. For instance, consider a pie chart representing a student's budget. If the student spends half of his or her money on rent, then the pie chart will represent that amount with a line through the center of the pie. If she spends a quarter of her money on food, there will be a line extending from the edge of the circle to the center at a right angle to the line depicting rent. This illustration would make it clear that the student spends twice the amount of money on rent as she does on food. A pie chart is effective at showing how a single entity is divided into parts. They are not effective at demonstrating the relationships between parts of different wholes. For example, an unhelpful use of a pie chart would be to compare the respective amounts of state and federal spending devoted to infrastructure since these values are only meaningful in the context of the entire budget.

> **Review Video: Data Interpretation of Graphs**
> Visit mometrix.com/academy and enter code: 200439

EFFECTIVE GRAPHIC REPRESENTATION

A graph should strip the author's message down to the essentials with a clear title and should be in the appropriate format. Authors may elect to use tables, line or bar graphs, or pie charts to illustrate their message. Each of these formats is correct for different types of data. For instance, if the text is about the differences between federal spending on the military and on the space program, a pie chart or a bar graph would be the most effective choice. The pie chart could show each type of spending as a portion of total federal spending while the bar graph would be better for directly comparing the amounts of money spent on these two programs.

INTERPRETATION OF INFORMATION PRESENTED IN GRAPHS, TABLES, CHARTS, AND DIAGRAMS

In most cases, the work of interpreting information presented in graphs, tables, charts, and diagrams is done for the reader. Usually, the author will make explicit his or her reasons for presenting a certain set of data in a certain way. However, an effective reader will avoid taking the author's claims for granted. Before considering the information presented in the graph, the reader should consider whether the author has chosen the correct format for presentation, whether the author has omitted variables or other information that might undermine his or her case. Interpreting the graphic itself is essentially an exercise in spotting trends. On a graph, for instance, the reader should be alert for how one variable responds to a change in the other. For example, if education level increases, does income increase as well? The same can be done for a table. Readers should be alert for values that break or exaggerate a trend; these may be meaningless outliers or indicators of a change in conditions.

DRAWING CONCLUSIONS BASED ON THE INFORMATION PRESENTED IN GRAPHICS

When readers are required to draw conclusions from the information presented in graphs, tables, charts, or diagrams, they need to know the importance of limiting these conclusions to the terms of the graph. In other words, the reader should avoid inferring unknown values from known values in the data to make claims that are not supportable. As an example, consider a graph that compares the price of eggs to the demand. If the price and demand rise and fall together, a reader would be justified in saying that the demand for eggs and the price are tied together. However, this simple graph does not indicate which of these variables causes the other, so the reader would not be

justified in concluding that the price of eggs raises or lowers the demand. In fact, demand could be tied to all sorts of other factors not included in such a chart.

SYNTHESIZING INFORMATION PRESENTED IN GRAPHICS

Graphs make information visual rather than only numerical or numerical and verbal. This enables you to see differences and similarities at a glance instead of having to compare or contrast numbers, e.g. those that go up and down over time. For example, a line graph clearly depicts overall patterns of amounts increasing or decreasing across designated time intervals. Bar graphs can also compare or contrast amounts occurring at the same time. Charts and tables can be used to summarize multiple, various numbers; however, looking at these generally requires more cognitive processing than looking at visual graphs. Synthesis involves combining information from multiple sources, including new information with prior knowledge. You can use existing knowledge to understand graphics, and combine new graphic sources with new verbal text for more complete understanding of a topic. As an example, if a text article reports that several business schools have recently lowered tuitions and redesigned curricula, and a graph shows new enrollment increases following these changes, it would be logical to connect these events.

SYNTHESIZING INFORMATION FROM A TEXT WITH EXISTING KNOWLEDGE

Readers often merge new information they encounter in text with their own existing knowledge; this merger results in the reader's ability to generate new insights, concepts, opinions, perspectives, trains of thought and other ideas. Through synthesis, they also boost their reading comprehension via cognitive processes of rephrasing new information in their own words and connecting it with what they already know. This improved understanding increases the likelihood that they will retain the new information and be able to transfer it to other contexts and generalize it across applicable situations. Retention, transfer, and generalization additionally reinforce the new information further. The process of synthesizing while reading by good readers includes pausing to gather their thoughts; identifying a text's main idea; rephrasing information in their own terms and responding; and combining reading with what they previously knew and responding to the results. Students may make notes of questions they have as they read, review the notes to see whether they have found answers in text, and look for any unanswered questions as they continue and finish reading.

GRAPHIC ORGANIZERS

A simple graphic organizer for comparing and contrasting two concepts, events, processes, or objects is a T-chart. The two sides of the top enable headings, with two vertical columns of characteristics. For example, with alligators and crocodiles as categories, one difference is identified under Alligators that bottom teeth are covered, and under Crocodiles that bottom teeth are exposed. T-charts can be expanded to include multiple columns for comparing more than two categories.

A Venn diagram uses overlapping circles to compare and contrast: commonalities shared by 2-3 categories appear in overlaps, differences separately in each circle.

A sequence of events chain connects boxes with arrows to depict chronological order in history or fiction. If arranged in a circle, connected end-to-end, they can display life cycles of organisms or other cyclical or recursive processes. Timelines are similar, but also clarify time durations between events.

Idea webs facilitate brainstorming. Students write a main idea or topic in a central circle with lines radiating out, ending in circles for secondary related ideas, optionally with additional lines drawn out to evidence supporting these ideas.

Review Video: <u>Graphic Organizers</u>
Visit mometrix.com/academy and enter code: 665513

INTERRELATING MULTIPLE PROBLEMS

Problems encountered in many human activities are as complex as the humans and activities involved, in large part because they are interrelated and interact. One example of this from the medical field is dual diagnosis of a psychiatric disorder and a substance abuse disorder. The patient not only suffers the impacts of two separate conditions; these also interact. This interaction can cause some symptoms to mask others or symptoms to overlap, complicating diagnosis and treatment. Also, disorders can exacerbate each other, and each promotes relapse in the other. Substance abuse can trigger psychiatric symptoms and disorders, while people experiencing psychiatric problems often abuse substances to self-medicate. Substance abuse withdrawal symptoms may mimic psychiatric disorder symptoms. Similarly, either or both of these types of disorders can lead to other problems, also interrelated with one another, such as social withdrawal or isolation, relationship or family problems, financial difficulties, school or work problems, and legal problems.

COMBINING AND MANIPULATING INFORMATION FROM MULTIPLE SOURCES

In order to solve a problem, we must first determine what information is needed to solve it, and then we must set about gathering that information. We must synthesize this information, combining what we find from multiple, varied sources and organize it toward our problem solution. This entails several steps: First, carefully examine each information source. Second, keep your purpose in mind as you read the information in each source. Next, identify which specific details in each source will facilitate your solving the identified problem. Finally, assemble these details from all sources: combine them to inform a solution to the problem. If the problem requires you to draft an essay response, here are some additional steps to follow: Take notes about the details to help yourself see how they are related, how you can combine them, and how they contribute to solving the problem. Organize these notes by making an outline, putting them into a graphic organizer, making lists, etc. Finally, write an explanation of the solution based on the facts and details you researched.

Special Report: GMAT Secrets in Action

This section will walk you through techniques that can help you answer specific types of questions. The following section will provide you with the opportunity to practice these skills in a practice test modeled after the GMAT.

Quantitative Reasoning Subtest

No calculators are allowed on this section.

SAMPLE PROBLEM-SOLVING QUESTION

Three coins are tossed up in the air. What is the probability that 2 of them will land heads and 1 will land tails?

- A. 0
- B. $\frac{1}{8}$
- C. $\frac{1}{4}$
- D. $\frac{3}{8}$
- E. $\frac{1}{2}$

Look through the following methods and steps for solving this problem.

REDUCTION AND DIVISION

Quickly eliminate the outcomes that you immediately know do not fit. Since there are 3 coins with 2 options each, there are in total $2 \times 2 \times 2 = 8$ possible outcomes for the set. Out of these, there is only 1 way of getting all heads, and only 1 way of getting all tails, so you can subtract those them: $8 - 1 - 1 = 6$. Thus, there are 6 remaining possible outcomes, and the probability of those 6 outcomes occurring is $\frac{6}{8}$. Because there are only 3 coins, all other combinations will either be 2 heads and 1 tail, or 2 tails and 1 head. Those remaining combinations both have the same chance of occurring, meaning that you can just cut the remaining probability in half, leaving you with a $\frac{3}{8}$ chance that there will be 2 heads and 1 tail, and another $\frac{3}{8}$ chance that there will be 2 tails and 1 head, making answer choice D correct.

RUN THROUGH THE POSSIBILITIES FOR THAT OUTCOME

You know that you have to have 2 heads and 1 tail for the 3 coins. There are only so many combinations, so quickly run through them all. You could have:

$$H, H, H \quad T, H, H$$
$$H, H, T \quad T, H, T$$
$$H, T, H \quad T, T, H$$
$$H, T, T \quad T, T, T$$

Reviewing these choices, you can see that 3 of the 8 have 2 heads and 1 tail, making answer choice D correct.

73

FILL IN THE BLANKS WITH SYMBOLOGY AND ODDS

Many probability problems can be solved by drawing blanks on a piece of scratch paper (or making mental notes) for each object used in the problem, then filling in probabilities and multiplying them out. In this case, since there are 3 coins being flipped, draw 3 blanks. In the first blank, put an H and over it write $\frac{1}{2}$. This represents the case where the first coin is flipped as heads. In that case (where the first coin comes up heads), 1 of the other 2 coins must come up tails and 1 must come up heads to fulfill the criteria posed in the problem (2 heads and 1 tail). In the second blank, put a 1 or $\frac{1}{1}$. This is because it does not matter what is flipped for the second coin, so long as the first coin is heads. In the third blank, put a $\frac{1}{2}$. This is because the third coin must be the exact opposite of whatever is in the second blank. Half the time the third coin will be the same as the second coin, and half the time the third coin will be the opposite, hence the $\frac{1}{2}$. Now multiply out the odds. There is a $\frac{1}{2}$ chance that the first coin will come up heads, then it does not matter for the second coin, and then there is a $\frac{1}{2}$ chance that the third coin will be the opposite of the second coin, which will give the desired result of 2 heads and 1 tail.

$$\left(\frac{1}{2}\right) \times \left(\frac{1}{1}\right) \times \left(\frac{1}{2}\right) = \left(\frac{1}{4}\right)$$

But now you must calculate the probabilities that result if the first coin is flipped tails. So, draw another group of 3 blanks. In the first blank, put a T and over it write $\frac{1}{2}$. This represents the case where the first coin is flipped as tails. In that case (where the first coin comes up tails), both of the other 2 coins must come up heads to fulfill the criteria posed in the problem. In the second blank, put an H and over it write $\frac{1}{2}$. In the third blank, put an H and over it write $\frac{1}{2}$. Now, multiply out the odds. There is a $\frac{1}{2}$ chance that the first coin will come up tails, then there is a $\frac{1}{2}$ chance that the second coin will be heads, and then there is a $\frac{1}{2}$ chance that the third coin will be heads.

$$\left(\frac{1}{2}\right) \times \left(\frac{1}{2}\right) \times \left(\frac{1}{2}\right) = \left(\frac{1}{8}\right)$$

Now, since these two situations are mutually exclusive, you can add their probabilities together.

$$\frac{1}{4} + \frac{1}{8} = \frac{2}{8} + \frac{1}{8} = \frac{3}{8}$$

Verbal Reasoning Subtest

SAMPLE READING COMPREHENSION QUESTION

Mark Twain was well aware of his celebrity. He was among the first authors to employ a clipping service to track press coverage of himself, and it was not unusual for him to issue his own press statements if he wanted to influence or spin coverage of a particular story. The celebrity Twain achieved during his last 10 years still reverberates today. Nearly all of his most popular novels were published before 1890, long before his hair grayed or he began to wear his famous white suit in public. We appreciate the author but seem to remember the celebrity.

Based on the passage above, Mark Twain seemed interested in:

- A. Maintaining his celebrity
- B. Selling more of his books
- C. Hiding his private life
- D. Gaining popularity
- E. Writing the perfect novel

Review the following methods of solving this problem.

KEY WORDS

Identify the key words in each answer choice. These are the nouns and verbs that are the most important words in the answer choice:

- A. Maintaining, celebrity
- B. Selling, books
- C. Hiding, life
- D. Gaining, popularity
- E. Writing, novel

Now try to match up each of the key words with the passage and see where they fit. You are trying to find synonyms and/or an exact replication between the key words in the answer choices and the key words in the passage:

- A. Maintaining—no matches; celebrity—matches in sentences 1, 3, and 5
- B. Selling—no matches; books—a match with *novels* in sentence 4
- C. Hiding—no matches; life—no matches
- D. Gaining—no matches; popularity—matches with *celebrity* in sentences 1, 3, and 5
- E. Writing—matches *author* in sentences 2 and 5; novel—a match in sentence 4

At this point there are only 3 answer choices that have more than one match, choices A, D, and E. However, choices A and D both have the same number of matches with the same word in the passage—*celebrity*. This is a good sign because the exam will often have two answer choices that are close. If two answer choices point toward the same key word, it strongly indicates that key word holds the "key" to finding the right answer.

Special Report: GMAT Secrets in Action

Now we can compare answer choices A and D and the unmatched key words. Choice A still has *maintaining*, which does not have a clear match, while choice D has *gaining*, which also does not have a clear match. While neither of those have clear matches in the passage, ask yourself what are the best arguments that would support any kind of connection with either of those two words.

- *Maintaining* makes sense when you consider that Twain was interested in tracking his press coverage and that he was actively managing the spin of certain stories.
- *Gaining* makes sense when you consider that Twain was actively issuing his own press releases; however, one key point to remember is that he was only issuing these press releases after another story was already in existence.

Since Twain's press releases were not being released in a news vacuum but rather as a response mechanism to ensure control over the angle of a story, it can be said that his releases were more about maintaining control over his image than gaining an image in the first place.

Furthermore, when comparing the terms *popularity* and *celebrity*, there are similarities between the words, but in referring back to the passage, it is clear that *celebrity* has a stronger connection to the passage because it is the exact word used three times.

Since *celebrity* has a stronger match than *popularity* and *maintaining* makes more sense than *gaining*, it is clear that answer choice A is correct.

PROCESS OF ELIMINATION

The process of elimination for this passage could follow these lines:

- A. Maintaining his celebrity—The passage discusses how Mark Twain was aware of his celebrity status and would take steps to ensure that he got the proper coverage in any news story and maintained the image he desired. This is the correct answer.
- B. Selling more of his books—Mark Twain's novels are mentioned for their popularity, and while common sense would dictate that he would be interested in selling more of his books, the passage makes no mention of him doing anything to promote sales.
- C. Hiding his private life—While the passage demonstrates that Mark Twain was keenly interested in how the public viewed his life, it does not indicate that he cared about hiding his private life; it does not even mention his life outside of the public eye. The passage deals with how he was seen by the public.
- D. Gaining popularity—At first, this sounds like a good answer choice because Mark Twain's popularity is mentioned several times. However, the main difference is that he was not trying to gain popularity but simply trying to ensure that the popularity he already had was not distorted by bad press.
- E. Writing the perfect novel—Though every author of fiction may strive to write the perfect novel, and Mark Twain was a famous author, the passage makes no mention of any quest of his to write the perfect novel.

SAMPLE CRITICAL REASONING QUESTION

The cost of producing radios in Country Q is 10% less than the cost of producing radios in Country Y. Even after transportation fees and tariff charges are added, it is still cheaper for a company to import radios from Country Q to Country Y than to produce radios in Country Y.

The statements above, if true, best support which of the following assertions?

A. Labor costs in Country Q are 10% below those in Country Y.
B. Importing radios from Country Q to Country Y will eliminate 10% of the manufacturing jobs in Country Y.
C. The tariff on a radio imported from Country Q to Country Y is less than 10% of the cost of manufacturing the radio in Country Y.
D. The fee for transporting a radio from Country Q to Country Y is more than 10% of the cost of manufacturing the radio in Country Q.
E. It takes 10% less time to manufacture a radio in Country Q than it does in Country Y.

Read over the following methods of solving this problem.

ELIMINATE CHOICES

When in doubt, eliminate what you can first. Go through each answer choice and see if you can eliminate it from consideration.

- Answer choice A mentions labor costs even though labor costs are not even mentioned in the question. Rarely will the GMAT try to trick you by bringing up an unmentioned variable; therefore, answer choice A can be eliminated.
- Answer choice B mentions manufacturing jobs, and answer choice E mentions manufacturing time, but neither variable was mentioned in the question. Thus, both answer choices can be eliminated.

Now you are down to just answer choices C and D, making your task much easier.

- Answer choice D states that the transportation fee is more than 10% of the cost of manufacturing the radio. However, if that were true, then the total cost of importing a radio from Country Q would exceed the manufacturing cost in Country Y, which cannot be true because the question clearly states that the importing cost is still less even after the transportation and tariff costs are added in. Thus, answer choice D is incorrect.

This makes answer choice C the default correct answer.

PLUG AND CHUG

Take some sample numbers and plug them into the problem. Rather than having to remember the relationships, writing them down with real numbers helps a lot of students understand the problem better. Use round numbers like 100 that are easy to use in calculations, especially with percentages. In this case, you could write:

Country Y—$100 is the cost to produce 1 radio
Country Q—$90 is the cost to produce 1 radio (10% less)

The question states that even if transportation fees and tariff charges are added to the cost of producing radios in Country Q, radios are still cheaper to import. Since that would mean that the total cost from Country Q must be less than $100 (the cost in Country Y), then the transportation and tariff costs must be less than $10. This is because the manufacturing cost is already $90, and $90 + any number greater than or equal to $10 would not be less than $100.

Since the upper limit of the transportation and tariff costs is $10, and $10 is 10% of $100, that means that the tariff costs alone would definitely have to be less than 10%, which makes answer choice C correct.

Data Insights Subtest

Calculators are allowed on this section.

SAMPLE DATA SUFFICIENCY QUESTION

If a real estate agent received a commission of 6% of the selling price of a certain house, what was the selling price of the house?

> (1) The selling price minus the real estate agent's commission was $84,600.
> (2) The selling price was 250% of the original purchase price of $36,000.

- A. Statement (1) ALONE is sufficient, but statement (2) ALONE is not sufficient.
- B. Statement (2) ALONE is sufficient, but statement (1) ALONE is not sufficient.
- C. BOTH statements TOGETHER are sufficient, but NEITHER statement ALONE is sufficient.
- D. EACH statement ALONE is sufficient.
- E. Statements (1) and (2) TOGETHER are NOT sufficient.

The following methods and steps for solving this problem are great strategies to use.

USE ALGEBRA

If the answer is not immediately apparent, creating an algebra problem allows you to logically dissect the problem and statements into pieces that can be put together to solve whether or not each statement is sufficient to find the answer to the question. Statement 1 can be converted into:

$$x \text{ (the selling price)} - y \text{ (the commission)} = \$84{,}600$$

This alone does not tell you enough, yet you do have another piece of information that you can plug in. The question told you that the real estate agent's commission was 6% of the selling price. Since we set the variable x as the selling price, that makes the agent's commission $0.06(x)$. This allows us to replace y in the equation above with $0.06(x)$. Our equation is now:

$$x - 0.06(x) = \$84{,}600$$

The variable x can be factored out, leaving $x(1 - 0.06) = \$84{,}600$ or $0.94(x) = \$84{,}600$. Solving for x gives us:

$$\frac{0.94x}{0.94} = \frac{\$84{,}000}{0.94}$$

$$x = \$90{,}000$$

This is the selling price, meaning that statement 1 is sufficient to answer the question, but what about statement 2? Statement 2 can be converted into:

$$x \text{ (the selling price)} = 250\% \times \$36{,}000$$

This becomes:

$$x = 2.5 \times \$36{,}000$$

$$x = \$90{,}000$$

This is the selling price, meaning that statement 2 is also sufficient to answer the question, making answer choice D correct.

Special Report: GMAT Secrets in Action

SINGLE VARIABLE LOGIC

A method that works even faster than setting up equations is using simple logic. Whenever you are able to create an equation, if you know that you will only have a single variable to work with, then you can solve for that variable. The first statement says that "the selling price minus the real estate agent's commission was $84,600." When you quickly look at this statement it appears that you will have two variables. However, once you realize that you can substitute the variable for the agent's commission with a 6% multiplier based on the selling price (using the information in the question), then you know that you are actually down to just a single variable, meaning this statement alone is sufficient to solve for the answer.

The second statement says that "the selling price was 250% of the original purchase price of $36,000." A quick view of this statement reveals that you are going to have a simple equation with only a single variable and will be able to solve for the answer, meaning that this statement is also sufficient.

Warning: Make sure that the single variable you have identified is the variable asked about in the question. In this question, you are asked for the selling price. Therefore, the single variable in each statement must be the selling price. Take care to not make this simple mistake!

SAMPLE MULTI-SOURCE REASONING QUESTION

Email #1	
From	Regional Sales Manager to Sales Team
Date	February 20, 9:06 a.m.
Subject	Urgent: Review of Quarterly Sales Targets
	Team,
	After reviewing our sales figures for the past month, I have noticed that our numbers are not on track to meet this quarter's targets. We need to increase our efforts immediately. I expect a significant push, especially in the high-demand regions. Let's focus on the Tech-Advance product line, which seems to have the most potential for growth.
	Best, John
Email #2	
From	Sales Associate to Regional Sales Manager
Date	February 20, 10:13 a.m.
Subject	RE: Urgent: Review of Quarterly Sales Targets
	Hi John,
	I've reached out to our contacts in the high-demand regions, and they're excited about the Tech-Advance products. However, they're requesting additional discounts to place larger orders. If we can offer a 10% discount, they're willing to double their usual orders, which could help us meet our targets.
	Thanks, Emily

Email #3	
From	Regional Sales Manager to Director of Sales
Date	February 20, 11:32 a.m.
Subject	Proposal for Discount on Tech-Advance Line
	I've discussed our sales strategy with the team, and there's an opportunity to significantly boost our numbers. By offering a 10% discount on the Tech-Advance line to key clients in high-demand regions, we could potentially double our sales for this quarter. I need approval on this discount strategy as soon as possible to capitalize on this opportunity. Looking forward to your response, John

Consider each of the following statements. Does the information in the three emails support the inference as stated?

Statement	Yes	No
The sales team has identified a potential strategy to meet the quarterly sales targets.		
The Tech-Advance product line requires a discount approval to proceed with the proposed sales strategy.		
The sales team expects to exceed the quarterly targets without offering any discounts.		

SKIM BEFORE DELVING

First, let's take a quick look at all the emails together. You want to get a sense of the overall picture without getting into the details yet. Our context for the emails is discussing sales targets and strategies.

Focus on Key Details: Go back and pick out the important details. In email #1, the manager mentions the Tech-Advance product line. Why is that important? Because it's directly related to the strategy the sales team is considering. In email #2, Emily talks about offering a discount to increase orders. These specifics are key to understanding the proposed plan. You are looking for numbers, names, and specific proposals to be the basis of the inferences you are asked to make.

Investigate: Now that you have identified the key details, we can dig deeper. How do these emails connect? The second email responds to the first, suggesting a solution to the problem raised by the manager. The third email is seeking approval for that solution.

Solving the Problem: Let us apply these strategies to answer the questions. The first statement asks if the sales team has identified a potential strategy to meet the quarterly sales targets. Yes, the team did identify a strategy involving the Tech-Advance line and potential discounts.

For the second statement, you are asked if the Tech-Advance line requires discount approval. Since John, the manager, asks for approval in email #3, the answer is "yes," the sales team does need approval to offer discounts.

Lastly, the third statement is a bit tricky—it's asking if the sales team expects to exceed the targets without discounts. If you look at the details, associate Emily's suggestion for a discount indicates the team needs it to boost sales, which means without the discount, the team does not expect to exceed the targets. So, for this one, your answer would be "no."

SAMPLE TABLE ANALYSIS QUESTION

Employee	Department	Sales in Q1 (USD)	Sales in Q2 (USD)	Customer Feedback Score (1-10)
John	Electronics	20,000	25,000	8
Linda	Home Goods	15,000	18,000	9
Raj	Electronics	22,000	22,000	7
Maria	Clothing	18,000	24,000	8
Lee	Home Goods	17,000	17,000	6

Which employee had the highest percentage increase in sales from Q1 to Q2?

A. John
B. Linda
C. Raj
D. Maria
E. Lee

USING EQUATIONS TO SOLVE THE PROBLEM

Understand the Table Structure: First, take a moment to understand the layout of the table. It lists employees, their departments, their sales in two different quarters (Q1 and Q2), and their customer feedback scores. This step is about getting familiar with the data you will be working with.

Calculate and Compare: For this question, you are interested in the percentage increase in sales from Q1 to Q2. To find this, subtract the Q1 sales from Q2 sales, divide that number by the Q1 sales, and then multiply by 100 to get the percentage. Then do this for each employee. Be careful not to rush. It is easy to make a simple math error, so take your time with the calculations. Also, make sure you are looking at the correct columns for Q1 and Q2 sales.

Solving the Problem: For John, the percentage increase is $\frac{25,000-20,000}{20,000} \times 100\% = 25\%$. For Linda, the calculation is $\frac{18,000-15,000}{15,000} \times 100\% = 20\%$. Raj has no increase, so his percentage increase is 0%. For Maria, it is $\frac{24,000-18,000}{18,000} \times 100\% = 33.33\%$. And finally, Lee has no increase so, like Raj, his increase is 0%. So, who has the highest percentage increase? It is Maria, with a 33.33% increase.

ESTIMATION AND COMPARISON

Instead of calculating the exact percentage increase for each employee, you can estimate the increases to quickly determine who has the highest. This works well if the numbers are significantly different. For instance, you can see that Raj's and Lee's sales did not increase at all, so they are out of the running. Between John, Linda, and Maria, Maria's increase from 18,000 to 24,000 seems to be the largest relative increase. You can quickly conclude Maria has the highest percentage increase without doing the math.

PROCESS OF ELIMINATION

You can eliminate options that are clearly incorrect. Raj and Lee had no increase, so they can be eliminated. Among the remaining three, since you are looking for the highest percentage increase and not the absolute value, you can determine that an increase from 20,000 to 25,000 (John) is not going to be as large in percentage terms as an increase from 18,000 to 24,000 (Maria). This narrows it down to either Linda or Maria. A quick estimation can lead you to the correct answer, which is Maria.

SAMPLE GRAPHICS INTERPRETATION QUESTION

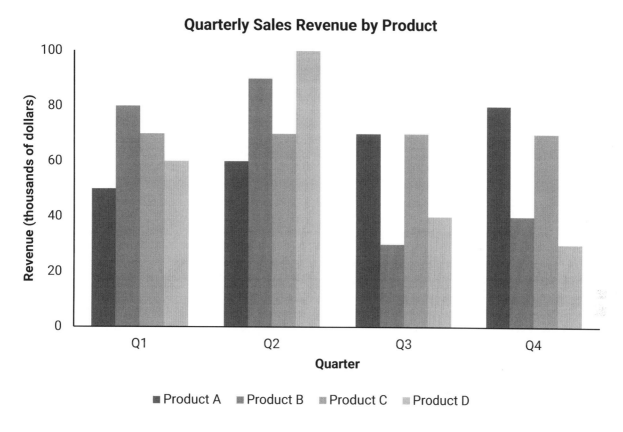

Quarterly Sales Revenue by Product

Based on the bar chart, which of the following statements are true? Select all that apply.

A. Product A's revenue increased every quarter, demonstrating a steady market growth.
B. Product B's sales were at their lowest in the fourth quarter.
C. The revenue for product C showed a variance of more than $10,000 between any two consecutive quarters.
D. Product D generated its highest revenue in the second quarter.

SOLUTION PROCESS AND STRATEGIES

Study Graph Characteristics: First, look at the graph provided. It is a bar chart showing quarterly sales revenue by product. There are four different products (A, B, C, and D), and each color represents one of them. The x-axis shows the quarters (Q1 through Q4), and the y-axis shows the sales revenue amount. Make sure you understand which color corresponds to which product.

Careful Reading of Statements: Now, carefully read each statement one by one. You are looking to see if each statement is accurate based on the data in the graph. Do not assume anything—only consider what you can clearly see in the chart.

Eliminate Incorrect Choices: If a statement does not match the data in the graph, you can eliminate it. For example, if a product did not increase in revenue every quarter but the statement says it did, then that statement would be incorrect.

Attention to Details: Pay close attention to the height of the bars for each product in each quarter. Small differences can be significant, especially when you are looking for things like the lowest sales or the highest revenue.

We can apply these strategies:

- For the first statement, check the bars for product A. Does the height of the bars increase from Q1 to Q4 without exception? This statement is true.

- For the second statement, compare the bars for product B across all quarters. Is the bar for Q4 the shortest among them? This statement is false.

- The third statement requires you to look for a difference of more than $10,000 in revenue between any two consecutive quarters for product C. Look for a significant change in the height of the bars from one quarter to the next. This statement is false.

- For the last statement, identify the tallest bar for product D. Is it in Q2? This statement is true.

Remember, the graph gives you visual information, so use it to validate each statement. If the visual evidence does not support the statement, then it is not true.

SAMPLE TWO-PART ANALYSIS QUESTION

In the region of the Andes Mountains, the Incas established a complex society known for its architectural feats, including Machu Picchu, as well as a network of routes that connected the enormous empire. The Inca Empire, the largest in pre-Columbian America, had its administrative, political, and military center in Cusco, not Machu Picchu.

The empire's history, recorded exclusively through oral traditions because the society lacked a written language, is filled with tales of advanced agricultural practices, religious ceremonies, and the worship of the sun god, Inti. Despite the challenging high-altitude environment, the Incas thrived without ever adopting the wheel for transportation.

Oral histories also recount the arrival of the Spanish conquistadors, led by Francisco Pizarro in the 16th century, who were the first Europeans to encounter the Incas. This marked the decline of the Inca Empire.

Given that all the information in the passage is correct, choose one statement that must be true about the Incas and one that must be false based on the provided information.

Statement	Must be true	Must be false
(1) Oral traditions were the primary method for documenting Inca history.		
(2) The Incas were completely isolated from other civilizations.		
(3) Machu Picchu was the only important political center of the Inca Empire.		
(4) The Incas possessed a complex system of laws and governance.		
(5) The Inca city of Machu Picchu was primarily used for religious purposes.		

Use Details and Cross Checks

Close Reading: Read the passage meticulously. Focus on identifying key facts and details that directly relate to the statements.

Cross-Referencing: Cross-reference each statement with the passage. Look for direct mentions or implications that confirm or deny the statement.

Elimination and Confirmation: Use the process of elimination for clearly incorrect options. Confirm the truth of statements with clear evidence in the text.

Now, we can apply these strategies to each statement:

- Statement (1): The passage explicitly states that Inca history was recorded exclusively through oral traditions because the society lacked a written language. This statement must be true.
- Statement (2): The passage clearly states that the arrival of the Spanish conquistadors, who were the first Europeans to encounter the Incas, marked the decline of the Inca Empire. However, it does not specify if the Incas were isolated.
- Statement (3): The passage specifies that Cusco, not Machu Picchu, was the administrative, political, and military center. Thus, this statement must be false.
- Statement (4): According to the passage, the Incas did have an administrative center, but details of a legal center are absent.
- Statement (5): The passage mentions Machu Picchu but does not provide conclusive evidence about Machu Picchu's main purpose, leaving room for speculation.

Special Report: GMAT Secrets in Action

85

GMAT Practice Test

Want to take this practice test in an online interactive format?
Check out the bonus page, which includes interactive practice questions and
much more: **https://www.mometrix.com/bonus948/gmat**

SCAN HERE

Quantitative Reasoning

No calculators are allowed on this section.

1. The number $2 + 0.4$ is how many times the number $1 - 0.2$?

    a. $1\frac{1}{3}$

    b.   2

    c. $2\frac{2}{5}$

    d. $2\frac{1}{2}$

    e.   3

2. What is the maximum number of $6\frac{3}{4}$-inch strips that can be cut from a spool of ribbon that is 10 yards long?

    a.   1
    b.   17
    c.   18
    d.   53
    e.   54

3. If $x^2 + 3x - 18 = 0$ and $x < 0$, which of the following must equal 0?

    I. $x^2 - 36$
    II. $x^2 - 2x - 3$
    III. $x^2 + 5x - 6$

    a.   I only
    b.   II only
    c.   III only
    d.   I and III only
    e.   I, II, and III

4. In a spelling bee, Anish's placement is both the 11th highest and the 25th lowest among all the spellers who participated. How many spellers participated in the spelling bee?

    a. 33
    b. 34
    c. 35
    d. 36
    e. 37

5. 32 is what percent of 80?

    a. 25%
    b. 32%
    c. 40%
    d. 44%
    e. 48%

6. The average of six numbers is 4. If the average of two of those numbers is 2, what is the average of the other four numbers?

    a. 5
    b. 6
    c. 7
    d. 8
    e. 9

7. Sheila, Janice, and Karen, working together at the same rate, can complete a job in $3\frac{1}{3}$ days. Working at the same rate, how much of the job could Janice and Karen do in one day?

    a. $\frac{1}{5}$

    b. $\frac{1}{4}$

    c. $\frac{1}{3}$

    d. $\frac{1}{9}$

    e. $\frac{1}{8}$

8. If $a = 4$, $b = 3$, and $c = 1$, then what is the value of $\frac{a(b-c)}{b(a+b+c)}$?

    a. $\frac{4}{13}$

    b. $\frac{1}{3}$

    c. $\frac{1}{4}$

    d. $\frac{1}{6}$

    e. $\frac{2}{7}$

9. Given the equation $\frac{3}{y-5} = \frac{15}{y+4}$, what is the value of y?

    a. 45

    b. 54

    c. $\frac{29}{4}$

    d. $\frac{4}{29}$

    e. $\frac{4}{45}$

10. A washing machine makes 85 revolutions per minute on the spin cycle. If the washing machine spends 15 minutes on the spin cycle per wash, about how many washes will it take to reach 100,000 revolutions (rounded to the nearest whole number)?

    a. 1,275

    b. 1,175

    c. 100

    d. 78

    e. 35

11. Rick scores 95%, 68%, 86%, 83%, 64%, 92%, and 79% on his math tests over the semester. When calculating students' semester averages, Rick's teacher disregards each student's highest and lowest score. What is Rick's average test score?

    a. 57.71%

    b. 75.5%

    c. 80.8%

    d. 81%

    e. 81.6%

12. What is the product of four squared and six?

    a. 22

    b. 28

    c. 55

    d. 96

    e. 106

13. A pilot traveled the first 1,500 miles of a 3,000-mile journey with an average speed of 400 miles per hour. At what speed must the pilot travel the remaining 1,500 miles to record an average speed of 500 miles per hour for the entire flight?

    a. $261\frac{2}{3}$ mph

    b. 600 mph

    c. $666\frac{2}{3}$ mph

    d. 800 mph

    e. 5,625 mph

14. If the fractions $\frac{5}{9}, \frac{6}{11}, \frac{1}{2}, \frac{9}{16}$, and $\frac{3}{5}$ are numbered from least to greatest, the second fraction of the resulting sequence would be?

    a. $\frac{5}{9}$

    b. $\frac{6}{11}$

    c. $\frac{1}{2}$

    d. $\frac{9}{16}$

    e. $\frac{3}{5}$

15. The length (L) of a rectangle is three times its width. What is the length of the diagonal in terms of the length (L)?

    a. $\frac{\sqrt{10}}{3}L$

    b. $\frac{10}{3}L$

    c. $\frac{10}{9}L$

    d. $\sqrt{10}L$

    e. $10L$

16. Jack and Kevin play in a basketball game. If the ratio of points scored by Jack to points scored by Kevin is 4 to 3, which of the following could NOT be the total number of points scored by the two boys?

    a. 7
    b. 14
    c. 16
    d. 28
    e. 35

17. Evaluate the following:

$$0.25 \times 0.03 =$$

    a. 75
    b. 0.075
    c. 0.75
    d. 0.0075
    e. 7.5

18. Dave can deliver four newspapers every minute. At this rate, how many newspapers can he deliver in 2 hours?

    a. 80
    b. 160
    c. 320
    d. 400
    e. 480

19. What is 20% of $\frac{12}{5}$, expressed as a percentage?

    a. 48%
    b. 65%
    c. 72%
    d. 76%
    e. 84%

20. If $a - 16 = 8b + 6$, what does $a + 3$ equal?

    a. $b + 3$
    b. $8b + 19$
    c. $8b + 22$
    d. $8b + 25$
    e. 25

21. Expand the following expression: $(y + 1)(y + 2)(y + 3)$

    a. $y^2 + 3y + 2$
    b. $3y^2 + 6y + 3$
    c. $2y^2 + 11y$
    d. $y^3 + 6y^2 + 11y + 6$
    e. $8y^3 + 6y + 8$

Verbal Reasoning

1. Consider the following statements:

> (1) All *A* are *B*.
> (2) Some *B* are *C*.

Which of the following is true?

- a. All *A* are *C*
- b. No *A* are *C*
- c. Some *A* are *C*
- d. No *C* are *A*
- e. None of the above

2. In 1781, a county court in Massachusetts heard the case *Brom & Bett v. Ashley*. What was unusual about the case was that the plaintiffs were both enslaved by John Ashley's family. They had walked out and appealed to a lawyer for help after Mrs. Ashley tried to hit Mum Bett's sister. Mum Bett, whose real name was Elizabeth Freeman, claimed that if all people were free and equal, as she had heard while serving at the Ashley table, slaves too were equal. The court agreed, basing their decision on the Massachusetts constitution of the previous year. The decision, affirmed in subsequent cases, led to the abolishing of slavery in that state. *Which of the following statements is most accurate?*

- a. Mrs. Ashley was probably just having a bad day when she tried to strike another person.
- b. Elizabeth Freeman's actions helped to gain women the right to vote.
- c. White people in southern states applauded the court's decision.
- d. The ideals of the American Revolution reached farther than the founders may have intended.
- e. All slaveholders in Massachusetts rushed to free their servants.

3. A recent exposé reported that a new series of television commercials makes deceptive claims about the health benefits of a new cereal. The reporter drew the conclusion that the commercials could cause consumers to actually choose a less healthful cereal for its supposed health benefits. *Which of the following choices would best reinforce the reporter's conclusion?*

- a. Television stations rely heavily on food commercials as a source of revenue.
- b. Television executives have little idea whether a particular commercial is true or false.
- c. Viewers depend on commercials as a way to understand the health benefits of new foods.
- d. Television commercials tend to distort information more than print ads do.
- e. All food ads are carefully screened by a panel of experts for accuracy before they are put on the air.

4. A widely believed anthropological theory states that the Hill People, an early culture on Mucky Muck Island, fought with and were eventually wiped out by the Lothars whose culture dominates the island today. More recently, however, anthropologists have proposed that modern Mucky Muck culture is more complex than they previously thought. The theory states that the Lothars, the Hill People, and several other tribes lived side-by-side for a long time and that the modern culture shows influences from several societies. *Which piece of evidence would most strongly support the more modern theory about the culture of the Mucky Muck Islanders?*

    a. Archaeological evidence shows that both the Hill People and the Lothars originated in Central Europe at least 10,000 years before they arrived on Mucky Muck Island.

    b. The Hill People and the Lothars had similar height, build, and facial features.

    c. A modern Mucky Muck myth incorporates a Hill People hero, one of the gods of the Lothars, as well as fertility rituals used by other cultures in the area.

    d. The Hill People culture remained a primitive hunter-gatherer culture, while the Lothars learned agriculture and advanced tool-making skills.

    e. The Lothars were willing to trade with strangers, while the Hill People were culturally insular and suspicious.

5. Victims of Marah's disease, a virtually unknown neurological condition, appear pain-free and content. Often, they also have a desire to engage in vigorous physical activities such as contact sports. Beneath it all, they are in great physical pain but have an inability to express it or act to reduce it, making diagnosis difficult. As a result, they are inaccurately diagnosed as very low on the pain scale, their discomfort level much lower than victims of severe sprains, despite the fact that sprains, although more painful, are temporary and comparatively easy to manage nature. *This passage makes the argument that:*

    a. The pain scale is not an accurate or adequate way to measure the physical discomfort of certain people, such as those suffering from Marah's disease.

    b. Sprain victims have more intense pain than Marah's sufferers, but they can manage their pain more easily.

    c. The pain scale seems to put more emphasis on intensity of pain than duration.

    d. Victims of Marah's syndrome are often unable to deal effectively with their discomfort.

    e. There needs to be more public awareness of Marah's syndrome.

6. Between 1980 and 1985, the incarceration rate of the poorest 20% of Americans decreased from 70% of the total prison population to 60%. During the same period, however, the incarceration rate for the poorest 8% increased from 18% to 35%. *Which of the factors below helps to explain this discrepancy?*

    a. Between 1980 and 1985, an estimated 20,000 more cops were put on the street.

    b. Between 1980 and 1985, prosecution of crimes of desperation such as petty theft increased by more than 50%.

    c. Between 1980 and 1985, many of the working poor were able to climb out of poverty.

    d. Between 1980 and 1985, prosecution of white-collar crime declined, leaving more rich criminals out of the justice system.

    e. Between 1980 and 1985, the incarceration rate for Americans overall was below 1%.

GMAT Practice Test

7. Shakespeare is the greatest writer of all time. This is because he wrote the greatest plays, and the greatest writer is the one who composes the greatest works. *Which of the following statements most effectively challenges the reasoning above?*

   a.   This argument disproves its own premise.
   b.   This argument uses ambiguous language.
   c.   This argument assumes what it claims to prove.
   d.   This argument introduces irrelevant evidence.
   e.   This argument fails to make a clear claim.

8. When the euro was introduced in January 2002, a single euro was valued at 88 cents in United States currency. In the summer of 2008, at one point it required $1.60 U.S. to buy 1 euro. In late October 2008, the euro fell to its lowest level against the dollar in two years. *Which of the following statements represents an accurate conclusion?*

   a.   The world in 2008 was headed for another Great Depression.
   b.   The dollar regained strength after significant devaluing against the euro.
   c.   The euro remains the world's strongest currency.
   d.   Investors need to keep buying stocks.
   e.   Globalization is a very bad idea.

9. All college students who play video games develop increased hand-eye coordination. All college students who major in the biological sciences make excellent doctors and surgeons. Everyone in Riley's study group, including Riley, is majoring in the biological sciences, and all of them except Riley play video games. Therefore, everyone in Riley's study group will make excellent surgeons. *What assumption is made in the above argument that is not explicitly supported in the argument's text?*

   a.   Riley and her study group peers intend to be surgeons.
   b.   Riley and her study group peers started as biological science majors.
   c.   Riley and her study group peers are college students.
   d.   Riley and her study group peers are good at video games.
   e.   The use of video games translates to an improvement in study habits.

Refer to the following for questions 10–13:

One of the key features of the music scene in the past decade has been the increasing popularity of outsiders, especially those with a career. In previous decades, amateur status was seen as a lower calling or, at best, a step on the way to professional status, but many musical insiders now believe that amateurs actually constitute an elite group within the music scene, with greater chances of eventual success. Professionals, once able to fully devote themselves to the advancement of their musical careers, now find themselves hamstrung by a variety of factors that were not issues even a decade ago, giving the edge to people who do not depend on music for a livelihood. A number of technological, demographic, and economic factors are to blame for this change.

Full-time musicians always had difficulties making ends meet, but these difficulties have been vastly increased by a changing music scene. The increased popularity of electronic music, mega-bands, and other acts that rely heavily on marketing, theatrics, and expensive effects has made it harder than ever for local acts to draw crowds. The decreasing crowds at coffee houses, bars, and other small venues leave the owners without the ability to pay for live music. Amateurs can still play the same coffee houses as ever, and the lack of a hundred-dollar paycheck at the end of the night is hardly noticed. Professionals, however, have to fight more desperately than ever for those few lucrative gigs.

An even bigger factor has been the rise of digital media in general and digital file sharing in particular. People have been trading copies of music for decades, but in the days of analog tapes there was always a loss. The tape one fan burned for another would be of lesser quality than the original, prompting the recipient to go out and buy the album. Now that music fans can make full-quality copies for little or nothing and distribute them all over the world, it can be very hard for bands to make any money on music sales. Again, this does not make much difference to amateurs, but it robs the professionals of what has traditionally been one of their biggest sources of revenue.

All of this results in a situation so dire for professional musicians that their extra experience often doesn't balance out their lack of economic resources. The amateurs are the only ones who can afford to buy new gear and fix broken equipment, keep their cars in working order to get to shows, and pay to promote their shows. The professionals tend to have to fall back on "day jobs," typically at lower rates and with less opportunity for advancement. Even those professional musicians who are able to supplement their incomes with music lessons, wedding shows, and other traditional jobs are often living at such a low level that they cannot afford to buy the professional equipment they need to keep the higher-paying gigs. A fairly skilled amateur, by contrast, may not have the same level of virtuosity but will be able to fake his way through most of what a professional does at a more competitive rate, which will allow him to play professional shows.

10. The author of this essay is mainly:
a. Arguing for a return to a climate more favorable to professional musicians
b. Examining the causes of the increasing success of amateur musicians over professionals
c. Revealing the psychological toll the current economy takes on professional musicians
d. Disputing the claim that unsuccessful professional musicians simply don't work hard enough
e. Comparing the relative contributions of professional and amateur musicians

11. Which of the following statements about musicians does the essay most directly support?
a. Bars and coffee houses should be willing to pay a fair wage to professional musicians.
b. The most popular professional bands have not been affected by the changes that plague most professional musicians.
c. It is much easier for amateur musicians to book shows now than it was a decade ago.
d. Professional musicians have recently lost some of their most important sources of income.
e. With the shrinking music scenes, it is nearly impossible for a modern musician to support himself on music alone.

12. In his discussion of professional musicians in the last paragraph, the author:
a. Indicates that amateurs deserve their new, higher status
b. Shows that in the current climate, professionals may not have the ability to purchase and maintain the tools that they need
c. Points out the decrease in the market for wedding gigs and lessons
d. Questions an assumption about the status of professional musicians
e. Predicts a decline in the number of professional musicians

13. According to the essay, amateur musicians are becoming more successful at both amateur and professional gigs because professionals:

    a.   Exclusively perform high-paying gigs and are unwilling to play in clubs

    b.   Are not able to relate to ordinary people as well as amateurs can

    c.   Have financial needs that they are not able to meet in the current musical climate

    d.   Are in an industry that is particularly susceptible to economic changes

    e.   Don't receive the same respect as people with more lucrative careers

Refer to the following for questions 14–16:

Although technological tools like polygraph tests, psychological theories, and interrogation techniques have resulted in slightly greater accuracy for law enforcement agents catching liars, it is still important to understand the nature of lies and check unfounded assumptions that can lead to unquestioning acceptance of false statements. Because intentional deception is one of the biggest obstacles to a successful criminal investigation, developing the ability to separate dubious or outright false statements from true ones has to be one of the main goals of every police officer and law enforcement investigator. In addition, an officer must be able to quickly sort out the possible repercussions of a false statement and the ways it can affect the rest of an investigation, should one slip by police screening. This is the only way to punish the guilty, exonerate the innocent, and do the most possible good in preventing future crimes.

The most difficult lie to catch is the half-truth. Half-truths are distortions constructed by using a seed of truth as a way to sprout a more convincing lie. A half-truth may incorporate intentional exaggeration or understatement, lies of omission, false implications, or outright lies mixed in with actual facts. Half-truths that slip past the detectives investigating a case are classified as either "smoke" lies or "mirror" lies. Smoke refers to half-truths that slow down an investigation by casting doubt on otherwise promising leads or angles of investigation. Mirrors are lies that manage to send the detective off in the wrong direction altogether, usually by linking a fact to a false supposition.

Most other lies are overt and intentional. Usually, they are told as a way for a suspect or witness to protect himself or his friends or, more rarely, to cast suspicion on a rival. In some cases, these sorts of lies can be compounded by overzealous or corrupt police who want to earn a conviction of a supposed perpetrator at any cost. Particularly in high-profile cases with gruesome details, this sort of lie results in more false convictions than any other type of distortion.

14. Which statement most accurately conveys the essay's main idea?

    a.   New police techniques have been ineffective at helping investigators catch liars.

    b.   The worst lies aren't outright lies; they're sneaky half-truths.

    c.   People in law enforcement need to be able to recognize lies to be effective and just.

    d.   There are only two primary types of lies.

    e.   Most overt lies are told to protect a suspect or a witness.

95

GMAT Practice Test

Mometrix

15. The essay's writer would be most likely to say that a police officer's ability to recognize both lies and half-truths is:
   a. Indispensable in a criminal investigation
   b. Difficult because of the sophistication of some liars
   c. The most important tool that law enforcement has
   d. Important only when investigating a crime
   e. Crucial, but beyond the abilities of most officers

16. According to the essay, "smoke":
   a. Is the most frequently told type of half-truth
   b. Never contains outright lies mixed in with truth
   c. Can slow down an investigation
   d. Is used to protect the guilty
   e. Sends detectives off in the wrong direction altogether

Refer to the following for questions 17–19:

Daylight Saving Time (DST) is the practice of changing clocks so that afternoons have more daylight and mornings have less. Clocks are adjusted forward one hour in the spring and one hour backward in the fall. The main purpose of the change is to make better use of daylight.

DST began with the goal of conservation. Benjamin Franklin suggested it as a method of saving on candles. It was used during both World Wars to save energy for military needs. Although DST's potential to save energy was a primary reason behind its implementation, research into its effects on energy conservation are contradictory and unclear.

Beneficiaries of DST include all activities that can benefit from more sunlight after working hours, such as shopping and sports. A 1984 issue of Fortune magazine estimated that a seven-week extension of DST would yield an additional $30 million for 7-Eleven stores. Public safety may be increased by the use of DST: some research suggests that traffic fatalities may be reduced when there is additional afternoon sunlight.

On the other hand, DST complicates timekeeping and some computer systems. Tools with built-in time-keeping functions such as medical devices can be affected negatively. Agricultural and evening entertainment interests have historically opposed DST.

DST can affect health, both positively and negatively. It provides more afternoon sunlight in which to get exercise. It also impacts sunlight exposure; this is good for getting vitamin D, but bad in that it can increase skin cancer risk. DST may also disrupt sleep.

Today, daylight saving time has been adopted by more than one billion people in about 70 countries. DST is generally not observed in countries near the equator because sunrise times do not vary much there. Asia and Africa do not generally observe it. Some countries, such as Brazil, observe it only in some regions.

DST can lead to peculiar situations. One of these occurred in November, 2007 when a woman in North Carolina gave birth to one twin at 1:32 a.m. and, 34 minutes later, to the second twin. Because of DST and the time change at 2:00 a.m., the second twin was officially born at 1:06, 26 minutes earlier than her brother.

96

17. According to the passage, what is the main purpose of DST?

a. To increase public safety
b. To benefit retail businesses
c. To make better use of daylight
d. To promote good health
e. To save on candles

18. Which of the following is not mentioned in the passage as a negative effect of DST?

a. Energy conservation
b. Complications with time keeping
c. Complications with computer systems
d. Increased skin cancer risk
e. Sleep disruption

19. The article states that DST involves:

a. Adjusting clocks forward one hour in the spring and the fall
b. Adjusting clocks backward one hour in the spring and the fall
c. Adjusting clocks forward in the fall and backward in the spring
d. Adjusting clocks forward in the spring and backward in the fall
e. None of the above

Refer to the following for questions 20–23:

Theodore Roosevelt first implied the term "muckrakers" to a group of journalists and writers who had exposed corruption in business and government in the early twentieth century. Roosevelt intended the term, borrowed from John Bunyan's *Pilgrim's Progress*, to be somewhat pejorative, but the muckrakers were very influential for a time and provided strong impetus to the ongoing Progressive Era reform movement.

Around 1902, a number of prominent magazines including *McClure's, Collier's, Cosmopolitan, Everybody's* and the *Arena*, began featuring crusading exposes or "muckraking" articles. Some of these pieces were later expanded into full length books. Among the best-known were Ida Tarbell's *History of the Standard Oil Company* (1902); Lincoln Steffen's *The Shame of the Cities* (1904), documenting corruption in municipal government; Samuel Hopkins Adams's *The Great American Fraud* (1906), lambasting the patent-medicine industry; and Ray Stannard Baker's *Following the Color Line* (1908), a pioneering expose of American racism.

A few muckrakers made their case in works of fiction. Upton Sinclair's *The Jungle* (1906), a fictionalized account of the Chicago meatpacking industry, was the best known of the genre, but David Graham Phillips was perhaps the most prolific of the muckraking novelists. Among his numerous works were *Lightfingered Gentry* (1907), on the insurance industry; *Susan Lenox; Her Fall and Rise* (1908) published in 1917), on prostitution; and many others.

The muckraking spirit also influenced some of the major novelists of the time, although usually in less tractarian form. Frank *Norris's The Octopus* (1901) and *The Pit* (1903); Theodore Dreiser's *The Financier* (1912) and *The Titan* (1914); and Jack London's *Iron Heel* (1908) all address the social consequences of unregulated capitalist expansion.

After about 1912, the muckraking movement abated. The public tired of the exposes, some of which seem sensationalized and overly sordid. But muckraking already had exerted a major impact on the reform movement and would influence the policies of President Woodrow Wilson. Indeed, Ray Standard Baker became an aide to Wilson and later edited a six-volume collection of Wilson's public papers (1926-1927). Assuming many different forms, the muckraking impulse continued to influence American journalism as the twentieth century wore on.

20. Which of the following statements about Muckrakers does the passage best support?

a. Muckrakers were viewed as criminologists during the early 1900s.
b. Muckrakers were exposing corruption during the Progressive Era.
c. Muckrakers were used by politicians during the 1900s to downplay social reforms.
d. The Muckrakers continued to have success following 1912.
e. Muckrakers had a background in detective operations and a passion for exposing the truth.

21. From the passage, it can be inferred the muckrakers fueled the Progressive Era. Which of the following sentences supports this claim the best?

a. After about 1912…
b. A few muckrakers made…
c. The muckraking spirit…
d. Roosevelt intended the…
e. Around 1902, a number…

22. Which of the following words best characterizes the content of the passage?

a. Cooperative
b. Degrading
c. Revealing
d. Conventional
e. Operational

23. Which of the following did not contribute to the rise of the muckrakers?

a. The Octopus
b. Journalists
c. The Jungle
d. The Pit
e. Pilgrim's Progress

Data Insights

Calculators are allowed on this section.

Data Sufficiency problems consist of a question and two statements, labeled (1) and (2), in which certain data are given. You have to decide whether the data given in the statements are sufficient for answering the question, using only the data given in the statements and your knowledge of mathematics and everyday facts (such as the number of days in July or the meaning of counterclockwise). In these problems, you must indicate whether:

A. Statement (1) ALONE is sufficient, but statement (2) alone is not sufficient to answer the question asked.
B. Statement (2) ALONE is sufficient, but statement (1) alone is not sufficient to answer the question asked.
C. BOTH statements (1) and (2) TOGETHER are sufficient to answer the question asked, but NEITHER statement ALONE is sufficient to answer the question asked.
D. EACH statement ALONE is sufficient to answer the question asked.
E. Statements (1) and (2) TOGETHER are NOT sufficient to answer the question asked, and additional data specific to the problem are needed.

The other question types will include further instructions if needed. They may have more than one selection required to answer the question fully.

1. The table below shows the percentage of students at several local high schools that are failing each subject.

School	Math	English	Science	Social Studies
Candlewood	12%	6%	11%	4%
Ridgecrest	13%	5%	10%	6%
Woodlands	9%	5%	10%	5%
West Hills	12%	7%	12%	3%
North Forest	8%	4%	9%	4%

For each of the following statements select *Would help explain* if it would, if true, help explain some of the information in the table. Otherwise, select *Would not help explain*.

Would help explain	Would not help explain	
○	○	Ridgecrest is a private school with high tuition costs.
○	○	North Forest has a 1 hour study block built into their schedule.
○	○	Woodlands has the highest percentage of students participating in extracurricular activities.

2. Data Sufficiency: In triangle ABC, is $\overline{AB}$ longer than $\overline{AC}$?

(1) $\overline{AC}$ is opposite angle B.
(2) $\overline{BC}$ is longer than $\overline{AC}$.

a. Statement (1) ALONE is sufficient, but statement (2) is not sufficient.
b. Statement (2) ALONE is sufficient, but statement (1) is not sufficient.
c. BOTH statements TOGETHER are sufficient, but NEITHER statement ALONE is sufficient.
d. EACH statement ALONE is sufficient.
e. Statements (1) and (2) TOGETHER are NOT sufficient.

3. A coach is dividing up players on his basketball team for a scrimmage. There should be 5 players on each team. The coach currently has 4 players assigned to each team. He wants team 1 to be stronger at shooting than team 2. He wants team 2 to have better dribbling skills and passing skills than team 1. Players are rated 1–10 in each of the three categories. Listed below is Player name (shooting rating, dribbling rating, passing rating).

Team 1	Team 2
Isaac (7, 8, 6)	Michael (6, 6, 7)
Timothy (7, 5, 7)	Tony (8, 8, 7)
Steve (8, 6, 8)	Chris (6, 7, 9)
Jordan (6, 8, 7)	John (9, 5, 6)

Select the player that could be added to team 1 to meet the coach's criteria and the select the player that could be added to team 2 to meet the coach's criteria. He averages each of the players rating to get a team rating. When selecting a player only take into account the opposite team's current rating (not the rating they will have after selecting a player for that team).

Team 1	Team 2	Player
○	○	Gordon (9, 9, 5)
○	○	James (9, 5, 4)
○	○	Caleb (8, 8, 7)
○	○	Howard (6, 8, 7)
○	○	Ben (5, 8, 8)

4. Data Sufficiency: Is line AB parallel to line CD?

(1) A transversal, intersecting the two lines, forms congruent corresponding angles.
(2) A transversal, intersecting the two lines, forms congruent alternate interior angles.

a. Statement (1) ALONE is sufficient, but statement (2) is not sufficient.
b. Statement (2) ALONE is sufficient, but statement (1) is not sufficient.
c. BOTH statements TOGETHER are sufficient, but NEITHER statement ALONE is sufficient.
d. EACH statement ALONE is sufficient.
e. Statements (1) and (2) TOGETHER are NOT sufficient.

5. Data Sufficiency: What is the average test score of Angela, Barry, Carl, Dennis, and Edward?

>   (1) The average of the test scores of Barry, Carl, and Edward is 87.
>   (2) The average of the test scores of Angela and Dennis is 84.

   a.   Statement (1) ALONE is sufficient, but statement (2) is not sufficient.
   b.   Statement (2) ALONE is sufficient, but statement (1) is not sufficient.
   c.   BOTH statements TOGETHER are sufficient, but NEITHER statement ALONE is sufficient.
   d.   EACH statement ALONE is sufficient.
   e.   Statements (1) and (2) TOGETHER are NOT sufficient.

6. The flowchart below represents a mathematical algorithm that takes two positive integers as the input and returns a positive integer as the output. Processes are indicated in the symbols in the flowchart.

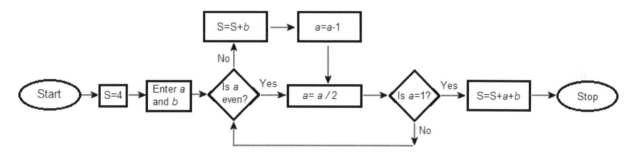

If 9 and 11 are entered as values for *a* and *b* respectively, then what is the value for *S* when you get to Stop?

   a.   20
   b.   27
   c.   28
   d.   32

If 19 and 4 are entered as values for *a* and *b* respectively, then what is the value for *S* when you get to Stop?

   a.   13
   b.   14
   c.   17
   d.   18

7. The table below displays 5 toy companies' production for dolls, action figures, and toy cars for the year 2014. Assume that these are the only toys the company produces.

Company	Total Dolls	Total Action Figures	Total Toy Cars
Pop Toys	2800	3500	3700
Wild West Toys	3000	3400	3200
Tots Toys	3500	3100	3500
Lots of Toys	3000	2900	3400
Uptown Toys	2700	2800	3100

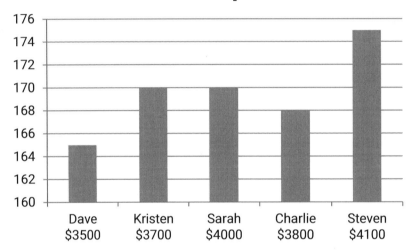

For each of the following statements, select *True* if it the statement can be shown to be true based on the information in the table. Otherwise, select *False*.

True	False	Statement
◯	◯	No one company produces more than 25% of the total dolls produced
◯	◯	Wild West Toys produced the largest volume of toys overall
◯	◯	Lots of Toys produced more toy cars as a percentage of total production than Tots Toys

8. Below is a chart of 5 employees and the number of hours they work per month. The number under their name is their salary per month.

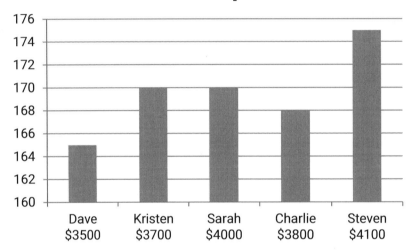

Hours worked per month

| | Dave $3500 | Kristen $3700 | Sarah $4000 | Charlie $3800 | Steven $4100 |

Select the expression below that best represents the calculation of their hourly wage. Then select the employee that is paid the most per hour. In the equations, *H* is hourly wage, *M* is monthly salary, and *T* is the number of hours per month.

Calculation of hourly wage		Paid most per hour	
◯	$M = \dfrac{H}{T}$	◯	Dave
◯	$H = \dfrac{M}{T}$	◯	Kristen
◯	$H = M \times T$	◯	Sarah
◯	$T = \dfrac{H}{M}$	◯	Charlie
		◯	Steven

9. Data Sufficiency: Given the sequences produced by the functions, $a_n = 2^n$ and $a_n = 2^{n+1}$, which sequence has a larger value for the 11th term?

      (1) n is a real number
      (2) n is a positive integer

  a. Statement (1) ALONE is sufficient, but statement (2) is not sufficient.
  b. Statement (2) ALONE is sufficient, but statement (1) is not sufficient.
  c. BOTH statements TOGETHER are sufficient, but NEITHER statement ALONE is sufficient.
  d. EACH statement ALONE is sufficient.
  e. Statements (1) and (2) TOGETHER are NOT sufficient.

10. A study done on 500 cats yielded the following results. Each symbol represents 20 cats.

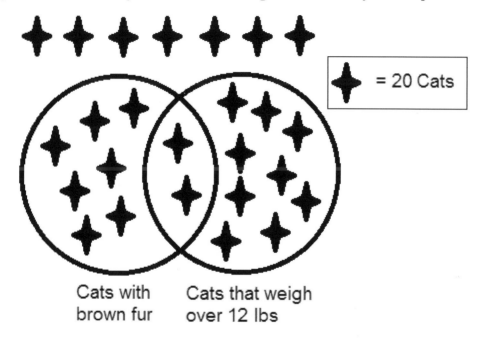

Cats with brown fur   Cats that weigh over 12 lbs

For the following statements select either *possible* if the statement is possible according to the results or *not possible* if it is not.

Possible	Not Possible	Statement
○	○	There were 210 cats with black fur.
○	○	There were 190 cats that weighed 13–15 lbs.
○	○	There were 155 cats that weighed 9–11 lbs and had brown fur.

11. Data Sufficiency: Does Jonathan get paid more than Deborah?

      (1) Alice gets paid more than Deborah.
      (2) Jonathan makes less money than Alice.

  a. Statement (1) ALONE is sufficient, but statement (2) is not sufficient.
  b. Statement (2) ALONE is sufficient, but statement (1) is not sufficient.
  c. BOTH statements TOGETHER are sufficient, but NEITHER statement ALONE is sufficient.
  d. EACH statement ALONE is sufficient.
  e. Statements (1) and (2) TOGETHER are NOT sufficient.

12. Data Sufficiency: If *q* is an integer between 2 and 9 inclusive and *q* is also the square root of an integer, what is the value of *q*?

    (1) *q* is even.
    (2) The cube root of *q* is an integer.

  a. Statement (1) ALONE is sufficient, but statement (2) is not sufficient.
  b. Statement (2) ALONE is sufficient, but statement (1) is not sufficient.
  c. BOTH statements TOGETHER are sufficient, but NEITHER statement ALONE is sufficient.
  d. EACH statement ALONE is sufficient.
  e. Statements (1) and (2) TOGETHER are NOT sufficient.

Refer to the following for questions 13–14:

Comets

Comets are bodies that orbit the sun. They are distinguishable from asteroids by the presence of comas or tails. In the outer solar system, comets remain frozen and are so small that they are difficult to detect from Earth. As a comet approaches the inner solar system, solar radiation causes the materials within the comet to vaporize and trail off the nuclei. The released dust and gas forms a fuzzy atmosphere called the coma, and the force exerted on the coma causes a tail to form, pointing away from the sun.

Comet nuclei are made of ice, dust, rock and frozen gases and vary widely in size: from 100 meters or so to tens of kilometers across. The comas may be even larger than the Sun. Because of their low mass, they do not become spherical and have irregular shapes.

There are over 3,500 known comets, and the number is steadily increasing. This represents only a small portion of the total comets existing, however. Most comets are too faint to be visible without the aid of a telescope; the number of comets visible to the naked eye is around one a year.

Comets leave a trail of solid debris behind them. If a comet's path crosses the Earth's path, there will likely be meteor showers as Earth passes through the trail of debris.

Many comets and asteroids have collided into Earth. Some scientists believe that comets hitting Earth about 4 billion years ago brought a significant proportion of the water in Earth's oceans. There are still many near-Earth comets.

Most comets have oval shaped orbits that take them close to the Sun for part of their orbit and then out further into the Solar System for the remainder of the orbit. Comets are often classified according to the length of their orbital period: short period comets have orbital periods of less than 200 years, long period comets have orbital periods of more than 200 years, single apparition comets have trajectories which cause them to permanently leave the solar system after passing the Sun once.

Stars

There are different life cycle possibilities for stars after they initially form and enter into the main sequence stage. Small, relatively cold red dwarfs with relatively low masses burn hydrogen slowly, and will remain in the main sequence for hundreds of billions of years. Massive, hot supergiants will leave the main sequence after just a few million years. The Sun is a mid-sized star that may be in the main sequence for 10 billion years. After the main sequence, the star expands to become a red giant. Depending upon the initial mass of the star, it can become a black dwarf (from a medium-sized star), and then a small, cooling white dwarf. Massive stars become red supergiants (and sometimes blue supergiants), explode in a supernova, and then become neutron stars. The largest stars can become black holes.

A nebula is a cloud of dust and gas that is composed primarily of hydrogen (97%) and helium (3%). Gravity causes parts of the nebula to clump together. This accretion continues adding atoms to the center of an unstable protostar. Equilibrium between gravity pulling atoms and gas pressure pushing heat and light away from the center is achieved. A star dies when it is no longer able to maintain equilibrium. A protostar may never become a star if it does not reach a critical core temperature. It may become a brown dwarf or a gas giant instead. If nuclear fusion of hydrogen into helium begins, a star is born. The "main sequence" of a star's life involves nuclear fusion reactions. During this time, the star contracts over billions of years to compensate for the heat and light energy lost. In the star's core, temperature, density, and pressure increase as the star contracts and the cycle continues.

13. For each of the following descriptions give either a *yes* or a *no* as to whether or not it describes comets.

Yes	No	Description
○	○	Have collided with Earth
○	○	Have an orbital period of only 150 years
○	○	Are formed when gravity causes parts of the nebula to clump together

14. Decide whether or not the following statements are true or false based on the text.

True	False	Statement
○	○	Both stars and comets can be seen with the naked eye.
○	○	Comets have an oval shaped orbit while stars have a circular shaped orbit.
○	○	A nebula and a comet are both composed of 97% hydrogen.

15. Data Sufficiency: What were the net proceeds from a fundraiser on the third day it was held?

(1) Net proceeds on the third day were $50,000 more than the first day.
(2) Net proceeds on the third day were three-quarters the second day's net proceeds.

a. Statement (1) ALONE is sufficient, but statement (2) is not sufficient.
b. Statement (2) ALONE is sufficient, but statement (1) is not sufficient.
c. BOTH statements TOGETHER are sufficient, but NEITHER statement ALONE is sufficient.
d. EACH statement ALONE is sufficient.
e. Statements (1) and (2) TOGETHER are NOT sufficient.

16. Data Sufficiency: What is the radius of circle *O*?

(1) The ratio of circle *O*'s area to its circumference is 2.
(2) The area of circle *O* is 16π.

a. Statement (1) ALONE is sufficient, but statement (2) is not sufficient.
b. Statement (2) ALONE is sufficient, but statement (1) is not sufficient.
c. BOTH statements TOGETHER are sufficient, but NEITHER statement ALONE is sufficient.
d. EACH statement ALONE is sufficient.
e. Statements (1) and (2) TOGETHER are NOT sufficient.

17. Complete each statement according to the information presented in the diagram. Daniel went for a walk through some woods near his house. For the first hour of the walk, he tracked his distance from home via a handheld GPS. The results are graphed below.

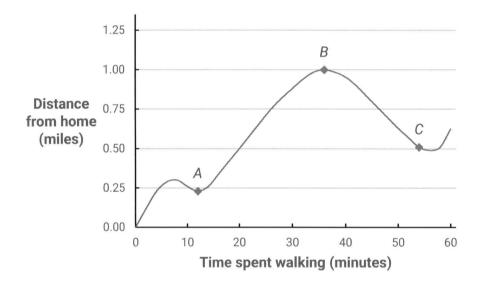

From point *A* to point *B*, Daniel moves approximately _____ more mile(s) away from his house.

a. 0.25
b. 0.5
c. 0.75
d. 1

From point *B* to point *C* he gets approximately _____ closer to his house.

a. 40%
b. 50%
c. 60%
d. 70%

GMAT Practice Test

18. Data Sufficiency: Brian is dividing 50 marbles into 3 groups. How many marbles are in the largest of the three groups?

    (1) The sum of the two smaller groups of marbles is equal to the largest group of marbles.

    (2) The smallest group contains 6 marbles.

    a.   Statement (1) ALONE is sufficient, but statement (2) is not sufficient.
    b.   Statement (2) ALONE is sufficient, but statement (1) is not sufficient.
    c.   BOTH statements TOGETHER are sufficient, but NEITHER statement ALONE is sufficient.
    d.   EACH statement ALONE is sufficient.
    e.   Statements (1) and (2) TOGETHER are NOT sufficient.

19. Complete each statement according to the information presented in the diagram. Refer to the pictograph below of a survey of students at a local elementary school. Each symbol represents 10 students in a sample of 200 students.

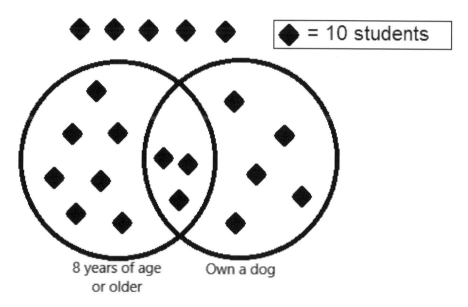

If one student is selected at random, the chance that student will be under 8 years of age is ____.

    a.   3 out of 4
    b.   1 out of 3
    c.   1 out of 2
    d.   4 out of 5

If one student is selected at random, the chance that student will be both under 8 and not own a dog is ____.

    a.   1 out of 3
    b.   1 out of 4
    c.   4 out of 5
    d.   2 out of 3

20. Data Sufficiency: Does y vary directly with x?

(1) The y-intercept of the linear equation, relating x and y, is 0.

(2) There is a constant rate of change in the value of y for each subsequent x-value.

a. Statement (1) ALONE is sufficient, but statement (2) is not sufficient.
b. Statement (2) ALONE is sufficient, but statement (1) is not sufficient.
c. BOTH statements TOGETHER are sufficient, but NEITHER statement ALONE is sufficient.
d. EACH statement ALONE is sufficient.
e. Statements (1) and (2) TOGETHER are NOT sufficient.

Answer Key and Explanations

Quantitative Reasoning

1. E: First perform the operations:

$$2 + 0.4 = 2.4$$
$$1 - 0.2 = 0.8$$

Next, solve the equation:

$$2.4 = x(0.8)$$
$$x = 3$$

2. D: First, convert 10 yards to inches: 1 yard = 36 inches, so 10 yards = 360 inches.

Next, convert the mixed fraction $6\frac{3}{4}$ to a decimal: 6.75.

Finally, divide: $\frac{360}{6.75} = 53.\overline{3}$

So, the maximum number of strips that can be cut is 53.

3. D: If $x^2 + 3x - 18 = 0$, then $(x + 6)(x - 3) = 0$. So $x = \{-6,3\}$. We are told $x < 0$, so $x = -6$.

I. $(-6)^2 - 36 = 0$ True

II. $(-6)^2 - 2(-6) - 3 \neq 0$ False

III. $(-6)^2 + 5(-6) - 6 = 0$ True

4. C: If Anish was the 11th highest speller, 10 participants placed higher. If Anish was the 25th lowest speller, 24 participants placed lower. Therefore, the total number of participants was:

$$10 + 24 + 1 = 35$$

5. C: This problem is solved by finding x in this equation: $\frac{32}{80} = \frac{x}{100}$.

6. A: A set of six numbers with an average of 4 must have a collective sum of 24. The two numbers that average 2 will add up to 4, so the remaining numbers must add up to 20. The average of these four numbers can be calculated: $\frac{20}{4} = 5$.

7. A: If it takes 3 people $3\frac{1}{3}$ days to do the job, then it would take one person 10 days: $3 \times 3\frac{1}{3} = 10$. Thus, it would take 2 people 5 days, and one day of work for two people would complete $\frac{1}{5}$ of the job.

109

![Mometrix]

8. B: Substitute the given values and solve. Resolve the parenthetical operations first.

$$\frac{a(b-c)}{b(a+b+c)} = \frac{4(3-1)}{3(4+3+1)}$$
$$= \frac{4(2)}{3(8)}$$
$$= \frac{8}{3(8)}$$
$$= \frac{1}{3}$$

9. C: Rearranging the equation gives $3(y+4) = 15(y-5)$, which is equivalent to $15y - 3y = 12 + 75$, or $12y = 87$, and solving for y, $y = \frac{87}{12} = \frac{29}{4}$.

10. D: First, determine how many revolutions the washer makes in one wash by multiplying $85 \times 15 = 1,275$. Then divide 100,000 by 1,275 to determine how many washes it will take to reach 100,000 revolutions. $100,000 \div 1,275 = 78.431373$. Round this number to 78, the nearest whole number. You may not be able to determine the precise answer, but you may be able to solve at least to the tenths decimal place and see that the answer is roughly 78.

11. E: The average of a group of terms is the sum of the terms divided by the number of terms. In this problem, the teacher disregards Rick's highest and lowest scores, so do not use 95% or 64% in your calculation. Add the remaining scores: $68 + 86 + 83 + 92 + 79 = 408$. Divide by the number of scores: $408 \div 5 = 81.6$.

12. D: Turn the word problem into an equation. Remember that product means multiplication:

$$4^2 \times 6 = 96$$

13. C: Use the Distance Formula: $distance = rate \times time$ AND $time = distance/rate$.

First half of trip: $1,500 = 400 \times time$, so $time = \frac{15}{4}$.

Second half of trip: $1,500 = rate \times \frac{distance}{rate} = rate \times \frac{1,500}{r}$.

Total trip: $3,000 = 500 \times time$, so the total trip time is 6 hours.

The total time of the trip is the sum of the times for the first 1,500 miles and the second 1,500 miles. So, $\frac{15}{4} + \frac{1,500}{r} = 6$. Solving for r, we multiply both sides of the equation by $4r$ and get:

$$15r + 6,000 = 24r$$
$$6,000 = 9r$$
$$r = 666\frac{2}{3}$$

14. B: We find the decimal equivalent of each fraction by dividing.

$\frac{5}{9} = 0.\overline{5}, \frac{6}{11} = 0.\overline{54}, \frac{1}{2} = 0.50, \frac{9}{16} = 0.5625$, and $\frac{3}{5} = 0.60$.

When we order these decimals from least to greatest, we find the second equivalent fraction to be $\frac{6}{11}$.

15. A: We are given $l = 3w$, so $w = \frac{1}{3} l$. The diagonal is the hypotenuse of the triangle with sides l and w, so we use the Pythagorean theorem.

$$l^2 + w^2 = d^2$$
$$l^2 + \left(\frac{1}{3}l\right)^2 = d^2$$
$$l^2 + \frac{1}{9}l^2 = d^2$$
$$\frac{10}{9}l^2 = d^2$$
$$d = \sqrt{\frac{10}{9}}l = \frac{\sqrt{10}}{3}l$$

16. C: Every possible combination of scores is a multiple of 7, since the two terms of the ratio have a sum of seven.

17. D: This is multiplication with decimals. It is often easiest to perform the multiplication on the numbers without the decimals and then figure out where to put the decimal in the final result. To do this, convert the decimals to fractions and then multiply:

$$0.25 \times 0.03 = \frac{25}{100} \times \frac{3}{100} = \frac{25 \times 3}{100 \times 100} = \frac{25 \times 3}{10,000}$$

$$\begin{array}{r} ^{+1}25 \\ \times 3 \\ \hline 75 \end{array} \qquad \frac{75}{10,000} = 0.0075$$

18. E: There are 60 minutes in an hour, so Dave can deliver 240 newspapers every hour. In 2 hours, then, he can deliver 480 papers.

19. A: Convert 20% to the fraction $\frac{1}{5}$, then multiply by $\frac{12}{5}$. The resulting fraction, $\frac{12}{25}$, must have both numerator and denominator multiplied by 4 to become a percentage.

20. D: Start by isolating a on one side of the equation.

$$a - 16 = 8b + 6$$
$$a = 8b + 6 + 16$$
$$a = 8b + 22$$

Next, add 3 to both side of the equation.

$$a + 3 = 8b + 22 + 3$$
$$a + 3 = 8b + 25$$

111

21. D: Expanding the expression requires you to multiply three algebraic expressions. When multiplying more than two expressions, multiply any two expressions (using the FOIL method), then multiply the result by the third expression. Start by multiplying:

$$(y + 1)(y + 2) = (y \times y) + (y \times 2) + (1 \times y) + (1 \times 2)$$
$$= y^2 + 2y + y + 2$$
$$= y^2 + 3y + 2$$

Then multiply the result by the third expression:

$$(y^2 + 3y + 2)(y + 3) = (y^2 + 3y + 2)(y) + (y^2 + 3y + 2)(3)$$
$$= (y^3 + 3y^2 + 2y) + (3y^2 + 9y + 6)$$
$$= y^3 + 3y^2 + 2y + 3y^2 + 9y + 6$$
$$= y^3 + 3y^2 + 3y^2 + 9y + 2y + 6$$
$$= y^3 + 6y^2 + 11y + 6$$

Verbal Reasoning

1. E: There is no way of determining whether any, some, or none of A are C.

2. D: Many of the founders were also slaveholders, even though they believed the practice was wrong. Response 1 is an assumption that cannot be supported. The second answer is false; Freeman's actions had no effect on women's suffrage though it did have an impact on slavery. White Southerners, the majority of whom were sympathetic to slavery, were unlikely to applaud the decision of the court; the third answer is incorrect. Response 5 suggests a broader response to the ruling than actually can be determined from the passage.

3. C: The question asks us to reinforce the conclusion that deceptive television commercials could cause consumers to be tricked into making a poorer health choice. For this to be true, we need to know that consumers actually believe what the ad says.

4. C: The modern theory states that the Lothars, the Hill People, and other cultures influenced each other, and that modern Mucky Muck shows the influence of more than one society. Therefore, we are looking for evidence of cultural cross-pollination. Choice A doesn't say that the cultures influenced each other, only that they both came from Central Europe. Choice B shows that the two peoples looked similar, but that doesn't mean that they had similar cultures or even a lot of contact—they may have evolved similar physical traits because they occupied the same environment. Choice D shows the two cultures diverging, not influencing each other. Choice E shows a difference between the two cultures but does not show them influencing each other. Only choice C shows cultural cross-influence. If a Mucky Muck myth incorporates a Hill People hero and a Lothar god, presumably the two cultures influenced each other to create the myth.

5. A: The author says that victims of Marah's disease "appear" to be comfortable but "beneath it all" are in pain. He says that they are "inaccurately" diagnosed as low on the pain scale. This shows that the pain scale is not an accurate way to measure Marah's disease.

6. B: While poor Americans were being incarcerated at a lower rate, the poorest Americans were being incarcerated more. Since the poorest are the most likely to commit "crimes of desperation" as a means to feed their families or take care of basic needs, it makes sense that increased prosecution would target them, while leaving the slightly less-poor unaffected.

7. C: This is an example of circular reasoning, in which the proof depends on assumptions which themselves have not been proven.

8. B: Although the nation faced recession, the U.S. dollar made a comeback in world currency during the fall of 2008. Response 1 cannot be concluded from the information given, which focuses solely on the dollar and euro rather than on the entire world. Response 3 is incorrect as well; the euro fell in 2008 against the dollar. The wisdom of buying stocks cannot be concluded from the information given; therefore, option 4 is not viable. The final option is a statement of opinion having nothing to do with the strength or weakness of the dollar.

9. C: The argument as written is intended to argue that the students mentioned will make excellent surgeons, but not that they must, or even intend to pursue that path. Additionally, the argument states that such students make excellent doctors and surgeons, which thus opens the possibility of not being a surgeon; thus, Statement A can be rejected. Statement B is invalid, because the argument states only that they are biological science majors, which has no bearing on their initial majors. Since the argument explicitly states that Riley does not play video games, the question of whether or not she is good is unanswerable, which makes Statement D inapplicable. Statement E cannot be known from the arguments above because we do not know the results of playing video games and its improvement in study habits or grades. So, Statement E can be rejected. While the first supporting statements reference college students, the argument does not explicitly state that Riley and her peers themselves are college students. Other educational institutions allow one to study, focus, or major in a subject before they attend a college or university. Thus, C is correct.

10. B: In the first paragraph of the essay, the author characterizes amateurs as "an elite group within the music scene" and states that there are several "technological, demographic, and economic factors" that account for them doing better than professionals. The tone of the essay is documentary—the author doesn't make any judgments about whether this is a good development or a bad one. He simply states that amateurs are more successful relative to professionals than they have been before and goes on to examine the reasons for this.

11. D: The key is the phrase "directly support." The essay needs to come right out and say the correct answer, not imply that it is true. Paragraph 3 says that digital file sharing "robs the professionals of what has traditionally been one of their biggest sources of revenue." Paragraph 2 provides less direct evidence, saying that many clubs that were once able to pay professionals now can't. Professionals have lost most of their income from both small clubs and recordings.

12. B: The second sentence in the final paragraph is a giveaway. If the "amateurs are the only ones who can afford to buy new gear and fix broken equipment, keep their cars in working order to get to shows, and pay to promote their shows," then the professionals must not be able to do any of those things.

13. C: The essay as a whole discusses how the current musical scene negatively affects professional musicians while leaving amateurs unharmed. The second paragraph, for example, discusses how professionals are no longer able to make a living playing small venues and must "fight more desperately than ever for those few lucrative gigs." The final paragraph states that, because of the effect on their finances, professionals are unable to maintain the gear and transportation they need to "keep the higher-paying gigs." It goes on to say that "a fairly skilled amateur ... will be able to fake his way through most of what a professional does ... to play professional shows." Therefore,

113

professionals are falling behind amateurs at small venues (which professionals can't afford to play because of the lack of pay) and at professional gigs (where professionals can't play because they can't afford professional gear).

14. C: The tricky thing about this question is that all the choices are true statements about things said in the essay. Only one, however, is the main idea. The best way to find it is to go to the first paragraph. In it, the author calls the ability to tell true and false statements apart "one of the main goals of every police officer." He goes further, calling this ability "the only way to punish the guilty, exonerate the innocent, and do the most possible good in preventing future crimes."

15. A: If there is one point that the author has repeated many times in this article, it is that police need to be able to investigate lies to conduct investigations. This is exactly the point explored in the explanation to question 33.

16. C: In paragraph 2, the author states that "smoke" lies "slow down an investigation."

17. C: The first paragraph states that the main purpose of DST it to make better use of daylight.

18. A: Energy conservation is discussed as a possible benefit of DST, not a negative effect of it.

19. D: The first paragraph states that DST involves setting clocks forward one hour in the spring and one hour backward in the fall.

20. B: The first paragraph talks about the muckrakers operating during the Progressive Era, and the rest of the passage discusses the specific corruption and societal ills that they brought to light.

21. D: This sentence states that the muckrakers "provided strong impetus to the ongoing Progressive Era reform movement."

22. C: The passage would be best characterized by the word *revealing*. The theme of the muckrakers was to reveal things to the public that were previously kept hidden behind closed doors.

23. E: Pilgrim's Progress was the book from which the term *muckraker* was taken, but the book itself did not contribute to the success of the muckrakers.

Data Insights

1. The correct selections are:

Would help explain	Would not help explain	
○	●	Ridgecrest is a private school with high tuition costs.
●	○	North Forest has a 1 hour study block built into their schedule.
○	●	Woodlands has the highest percentage of students participating in extracurricular activities.

The fact that Ridgecrest is a private school or has high tuition costs has no correlation to student's grades. Since North Forest has a built-in study block this would help explain why they have some of the lowest failure rates in the area. Having more students participate in extracurricular activities

could take away from their study time but since Woodlands still has low failure rates there seems to be no correlation.

2. E: The statements simply indicate the placement of the vertices of the triangle and the fact that $\overline{BC}$ is longer than $\overline{AC}$. It cannot be determined, from the given information, whether or not $\overline{AB}$ is longer than $\overline{AC}$. In order to make such a deduction, the statements would need to indicate the angle measures of each angle.

3. The correct selections are:

Team 1	Team 2	Player
○	○	Gordon (9, 9, 5)
●	○	James (9, 5, 4)
○	○	Caleb (8, 8, 7)
○	○	Howard (6, 8, 7)
○	●	Ben (5, 8, 8)

James will get Team 1's shooting average higher than Team 2 while getting their passing and dribbling average lower. Ben will raise Team 2's passing and dribbling average while keeping their shooting average lower than Team 1.

4. D: By definition, two lines are parallel, if a transversal, intersecting the lines, forms congruent corresponding angles or congruent alternate interior angles. Therefore, the correct answer is D; each statement ALONE is sufficient.

5. C: As long as the sum of all five test scores can be calculated, it will be possible to calculate the average score. Therefore, the correct answer is C; BOTH statements TOGETHER are sufficient, but NEITHER statement ALONE is sufficient.

6. B, C: In the first problem, a is 9 and b is 11. If you follow the diagram, you should perform the following operations:

Step	Decision/Action	S	a	b
$S = 4$	$S = 4$	4		
Enter a and b		4	9	11
Is a even?	No	4	9	11
$S = S + b$	$S = 4 + 11 = 15$	15	9	11
$a = a - 1$	$a = 9 - 1 = 8$	15	8	11
$a = \dfrac{a}{2}$	$a = \dfrac{8}{2} = 4$	15	4	11
Is $a = 1$?	No	15	4	11
Is a even?	Yes	15	4	11
$a = \dfrac{a}{2}$	$a = \dfrac{4}{2} = 2$	15	2	11
Is $a = 1$?	No	15	2	11

Step	Decision/Action	S	a	b
Is a even?	Yes	15	2	11
$a = \dfrac{a}{2}$	$a = \dfrac{2}{2} = 1$	15	1	11
Is $a = 1$?	Yes	15	1	11
$S = S + a + b$	$S = 15 + 1 + 11 = 27$	27	1	11

In the second problem, a is 19 and b is 4. If you follow the diagram, you should perform the following operations:

Step	Decision/Action	S	a	b
$S = 4$	$S = 4$	4		
Enter a and b		4	19	4
Is a even?	No	4	19	4
$S = S + b$	$S = 4 + 4 = 8$	8	19	4
$a = a - 1$	$a = 9 - 1 = 8$	8	18	4
$a = \dfrac{a}{2}$	$a = \dfrac{8}{2} = 4$	8	9	4
Is $a = 1$?	No	8	9	4
Is a even?	No	8	9	4
$S = S + b$	$S = 8 + 4 = 12$	12	9	4
$a = a - 1$	$a = 9 - 1 = 8$	12	8	4
$a = \dfrac{a}{2}$	$a = \dfrac{8}{2} = 4$	12	4	4
Is $a = 1$?	No	12	4	4
Is a even?	Yes	12	4	4
$a = \dfrac{a}{2}$	$a = \dfrac{4}{2} = 2$	12	2	4
Is $a = 1$?	No	12	2	4
Is a even?	Yes	12	2	4
$a = \dfrac{a}{2}$	$a = \dfrac{2}{2} = 1$	12	1	4
Is $a = 1$?	Yes	12	1	4
$S = S + a + b$	$S = 12 + 1 + 4 = 17$	17	1	4

7. The correct selections are:

True	False	Statement
●	○	No one company produces more than 25% of the total dolls produced
○	●	Wild West Toys produced the largest volume of toys overall
●	○	Lots of Toys produced more toy cars as a percentage of total production than Tots Toys

The total number of dolls produced can be found by adding up each company's production to get 15,000 total dolls produced. Since Tots Toys produced the most dolls they are the only company that needs to be checked. $\left(\dfrac{3,500}{15,000}\right) \times 100 = 23.33\%$. So, they produce less than 25% and this statement is true. To check the next statement first find Wild West Toys total production, which is

9,600. Then compare that to the total production of all other companies. If even one of them produced more toys, then the statement is false. Tots Toys produced 10,100 so this statement is false. For the last statement first find the percentage of total production for toy cars for both companies. Lots of Toys would be $\left(\frac{3,400}{9,300}\right) \times 100 \approx 36.56\%$, and Tots Toys would be $\left(\frac{3,500}{10,100}\right) \times 100 \approx 34.65\%$. So, this would be a true statement.

8. The correct selections are:

Calculation of hourly wage	
○	$M = \frac{H}{T}$
●	$H = \frac{M}{T}$
○	$H = M \times T$
○	$T = \frac{H}{M}$

Paid most per hour	
○	Dave
○	Kristen
●	Sarah
○	Charlie
○	Steven

The hourly wage is the amount of money they make per hour. So, the calculation should be total money divided by total hours, or $H = \frac{M}{T}$. Once you have this calculation you can perform it on each employee to see who make the most per hour. It will show that Sarah at approximately $23.53 makes the most per hour.

9. D: For any real number or positive integer, the sequence, $a_n = 2^{n+1}$, will have a larger value for the 11th term, since the exponent of n, has 1 added to it. The exponent on the base will always be larger in this sequence than in the other sequence, resulting in a larger value of each term.

10. The correct selections are:

Possible	Not Possible	Statement
●	○	There were 210 cats with black fur
●	○	There were 190 cats that weighed 13–15 lbs
○	●	There were 155 cats that weighed 9–11 lbs and had brown fur

The only information given about fur color is that there were 180 cats with brown fur. This means that there were 320 cats with some other color fur. So, it is possible that 210 cats had black fur. The only information given about weight is that 220 cats weighed over 12 lbs and the remaining 280 weigh less than 12 lbs. This means that of those 220 cats that weighed over 12 lbs it is possible for 190 of them to weigh between 13 and 15 lbs. It is shown that there are 280 cats that weigh less than 12 lbs but only 140 of those had brown fur. So, it is not possible for 155 cats to weigh between 9 and 11 lbs and have brown fur.

11. E: Statements (1) and (2) establish only that Alice is paid more than both Jonathan and Deborah; they do not indicate which of these latter two is paid more. Therefore, the correct answer is E; Statements (1) and (2) TOGETHER are not sufficient.

12. B: The even integers between 2 and 9 inclusive that are the square root of some integer are 2, 4, 6, and 8. Statement (1) is not sufficient. Of the integers 2 through 9, only 8 has a cube root that is an integer, so statement (2) is sufficient. Therefore, the correct answer is B; Statement (2) ALONE is sufficient, but statement (1) is not sufficient.

13. The correct selections are:

Yes	No	Description
●	○	Have collided with Earth
○	●	Have an orbital period of only 150 years
○	●	Are formed when gravity causes parts of the nebula to clump together

This can be determined from reading both of the passages. At the beginning of paragraph 5 in the text about comets it states that they have collided with earth. In the next paragraph it discusses their orbital period. It says they can have both a short and long orbital period so there is no one specific length of their orbital period. The part about gravity causing parts of a nebula to clump together is discussed in the text about stars.

14. The correct selections are:

True	False	Statement
●	○	Both stars and comets can be seen with the naked eye.
○	●	Comets have an oval shaped orbit while stars have a circular shaped orbit.
○	●	A nebula and a comet are both composed of 97% hydrogen.

Even though it states that there is only around one comet visible to the naked eye per year that still makes the first statement true. It does state that comets have an oval shaped orbit but does not say anything about a star having a circular shaped orbit or even orbiting at all. It is stated that a nebula is composed of 97% hydrogen but there is no mention of the composition of a comet.

15. E: Statement (1) does not give us the net proceeds total for the first day, and statement (2) does not give us the net proceeds total for the second day, so neither is sufficient. Without the total net proceeds for either the first or the second day, we are unable to find the net proceeds for the third day from the given information. Therefore, the correct answer is E; Statements (1) and (2) TOGETHER are not sufficient.

16. D: The formula for the area of a circle is $A = \pi r^2$ and the formula for the circumference of a circle is $C = 2\pi r$. So, the ratio of A to C is $\frac{\pi r^2}{2\pi r} = \frac{r}{2}$. Setting this ratio equal to 2, we get $r = 4$, so (1) is sufficient. The formula for the area of a circle is $A = \pi r^2$. Setting this equal to 16π, we get $16\pi = \pi r^2$, or $r^2 = 16$. So, $r = \{4, -4\}$, but the radius must be positive. Thus, $r = 4$ and (2) is also sufficient. Therefore, the correct answer is D; EACH statement ALONE is sufficient.

17. C, B: From Point A to Point B he moves from approximately 0.25 miles away to approximately 1 mile away. This means that he moves approximately 0.75 more miles away from his house.

From Point B to Point C he moves from approximately 1 mile away to approximately 0.5 miles away. There is a difference of approximately 0.5 miles.

$$\frac{1 \text{ mi} - 0.5 \text{ mi}}{1 \text{ mi}} \times 100\% = 50\%$$

18. A: Statement (1) establishes that the largest group constitutes half of the total amount of marbles, which means it must be equal to 25 marbles. So, statement (1) is sufficient on its own. Statement (2) does not provide enough information to infer the exact size of the largest group, so it is not sufficient. Therefore, the correct answer is A; statement (1) ALONE is sufficient, but statement (2) is not sufficient.

19. C, B: To find the chance that a student will be 8 years of age or under, first count all of the symbols not contained in the 8 years of age or older circle. There 10 are of the 20 not in the 8 years of age or older circle. This can be reduced to 1 out of 2.

To find the chance that a student is both under 8 years of age and does not own a dog, count all of the symbols outside of both circles. There are 5 of the 20 that are not in either circle. This can be reduced to 1 out of 4.

20. A: When y varies directly with x, the relationship is proportional, meaning the graph of the relationship passes through the origin, (0,0), indicating a y-intercept of 0. In other words, no constant amount is added to or subtracted from the term, containing the slope of the line. This means that statement (1) is sufficient. Statement (2) implies that the relationship is linear, with the constant rate of change noted. However, not all linear relationships are proportional. Such lines have y-intercepts, other than (0,0). Note that not all linear relationships are proportional, but all proportional relationships are linear. Therefore, the correct answer is A; statement (1) ALONE is sufficient, but statement (2) is not sufficient.

Answer Key and Explanations

How to Overcome Test Anxiety

Just the thought of taking a test is enough to make most people a little nervous. A test is an important event that can have a long-term impact on your future, so it's important to take it seriously and it's natural to feel anxious about performing well. But just because anxiety is normal, that doesn't mean that it's helpful in test taking, or that you should simply accept it as part of your life. Anxiety can have a variety of effects. These effects can be mild, like making you feel slightly nervous, or severe, like blocking your ability to focus or remember even a simple detail.

If you experience test anxiety—whether severe or mild—it's important to know how to beat it. To discover this, first you need to understand what causes test anxiety.

Causes of Test Anxiety

While we often think of anxiety as an uncontrollable emotional state, it can actually be caused by simple, practical things. One of the most common causes of test anxiety is that a person does not feel adequately prepared for their test. This feeling can be the result of many different issues such as poor study habits or lack of organization, but the most common culprit is time management. Starting to study too late, failing to organize your study time to cover all of the material, or being distracted while you study will mean that you're not well prepared for the test. This may lead to cramming the night before, which will cause you to be physically and mentally exhausted for the test. Poor time management also contributes to feelings of stress, fear, and hopelessness as you realize you are not well prepared but don't know what to do about it.

Other times, test anxiety is not related to your preparation for the test but comes from unresolved fear. This may be a past failure on a test, or poor performance on tests in general. It may come from comparing yourself to others who seem to be performing better or from the stress of living up to expectations. Anxiety may be driven by fears of the future—how failure on this test would affect your educational and career goals. These fears are often completely irrational, but they can still negatively impact your test performance.

Elements of Test Anxiety

As mentioned earlier, test anxiety is considered to be an emotional state, but it has physical and mental components as well. Sometimes you may not even realize that you are suffering from test anxiety until you notice the physical symptoms. These can include trembling hands, rapid heartbeat, sweating, nausea, and tense muscles. Extreme anxiety may lead to fainting or vomiting. Obviously, any of these symptoms can have a negative impact on testing. It is important to recognize them as soon as they begin to occur so that you can address the problem before it damages your performance.

The mental components of test anxiety include trouble focusing and inability to remember learned information. During a test, your mind is on high alert, which can help you recall information and stay focused for an extended period of time. However, anxiety interferes with your mind's natural processes, causing you to blank out, even on the questions you know well. The strain of testing during anxiety makes it difficult to stay focused, especially on a test that may take several hours. Extreme anxiety can take a huge mental toll, making it difficult not only to recall test information but even to understand the test questions or pull your thoughts together.

120

Effects of Test Anxiety

Test anxiety is like a disease—if left untreated, it will get progressively worse. Anxiety leads to poor performance, and this reinforces the feelings of fear and failure, which in turn lead to poor performances on subsequent tests. It can grow from a mild nervousness to a crippling condition. If allowed to progress, test anxiety can have a big impact on your schooling, and consequently on your future.

Test anxiety can spread to other parts of your life. Anxiety on tests can become anxiety in any stressful situation, and blanking on a test can turn into panicking in a job situation. But fortunately, you don't have to let anxiety rule your testing and determine your grades. There are a number of relatively simple steps you can take to move past anxiety and function normally on a test and in the rest of life.

Physical Steps for Beating Test Anxiety

While test anxiety is a serious problem, the good news is that it can be overcome. It doesn't have to control your ability to think and remember information. While it may take time, you can begin taking steps today to beat anxiety.

Just as your first hint that you may be struggling with anxiety comes from the physical symptoms, the first step to treating it is also physical. Rest is crucial for having a clear, strong mind. If you are tired, it is much easier to give in to anxiety. But if you establish good sleep habits, your body and mind will be ready to perform optimally, without the strain of exhaustion. Additionally, sleeping well helps you to retain information better, so you're more likely to recall the answers when you see the test questions.

Getting good sleep means more than going to bed on time. It's important to allow your brain time to relax. Take study breaks from time to time so it doesn't get overworked, and don't study right before bed. Take time to rest your mind before trying to rest your body, or you may find it difficult to fall asleep.

Along with sleep, other aspects of physical health are important in preparing for a test. Good nutrition is vital for good brain function. Sugary foods and drinks may give a burst of energy but this burst is followed by a crash, both physically and emotionally. Instead, fuel your body with protein and vitamin-rich foods.

Also, drink plenty of water. Dehydration can lead to headaches and exhaustion, especially if your brain is already under stress from the rigors of the test. Particularly if your test is a long one, drink water during the breaks. And if possible, take an energy-boosting snack to eat between sections.

Along with sleep and diet, a third important part of physical health is exercise. Maintaining a steady workout schedule is helpful, but even taking 5-minute study breaks to walk can help get your blood pumping faster and clear your head. Exercise also releases endorphins, which contribute to a positive feeling and can help combat test anxiety.

When you nurture your physical health, you are also contributing to your mental health. If your body is healthy, your mind is much more likely to be healthy as well. So take time to rest, nourish your body with healthy food and water, and get moving as much as possible. Taking these physical steps will make you stronger and more able to take the mental steps necessary to overcome test anxiety.

121

Mental Steps for Beating Test Anxiety

Working on the mental side of test anxiety can be more challenging, but as with the physical side, there are clear steps you can take to overcome it. As mentioned earlier, test anxiety often stems from lack of preparation, so the obvious solution is to prepare for the test. Effective studying may be the most important weapon you have for beating test anxiety, but you can and should employ several other mental tools to combat fear.

First, boost your confidence by reminding yourself of past success—tests or projects that you aced. If you're putting as much effort into preparing for this test as you did for those, there's no reason you should expect to fail here. Work hard to prepare; then trust your preparation.

Second, surround yourself with encouraging people. It can be helpful to find a study group, but be sure that the people you're around will encourage a positive attitude. If you spend time with others who are anxious or cynical, this will only contribute to your own anxiety. Look for others who are motivated to study hard from a desire to succeed, not from a fear of failure.

Third, reward yourself. A test is physically and mentally tiring, even without anxiety, and it can be helpful to have something to look forward to. Plan an activity following the test, regardless of the outcome, such as going to a movie or getting ice cream.

When you are taking the test, if you find yourself beginning to feel anxious, remind yourself that you know the material. Visualize successfully completing the test. Then take a few deep, relaxing breaths and return to it. Work through the questions carefully but with confidence, knowing that you are capable of succeeding.

Developing a healthy mental approach to test taking will also aid in other areas of life. Test anxiety affects more than just the actual test—it can be damaging to your mental health and even contribute to depression. It's important to beat test anxiety before it becomes a problem for more than testing.

Study Strategy

Being prepared for the test is necessary to combat anxiety, but what does being prepared look like? You may study for hours on end and still not feel prepared. What you need is a strategy for test prep. The next few pages outline our recommended steps to help you plan out and conquer the challenge of preparation.

STEP 1: SCOPE OUT THE TEST

Learn everything you can about the format (multiple choice, essay, etc.) and what will be on the test. Gather any study materials, course outlines, or sample exams that may be available. Not only will this help you to prepare, but knowing what to expect can help to alleviate test anxiety.

STEP 2: MAP OUT THE MATERIAL

Look through the textbook or study guide and make note of how many chapters or sections it has. Then divide these over the time you have. For example, if a book has 15 chapters and you have five days to study, you need to cover three chapters each day. Even better, if you have the time, leave an extra day at the end for overall review after you have gone through the material in depth.

If time is limited, you may need to prioritize the material. Look through it and make note of which sections you think you already have a good grasp on, and which need review. While you are studying, skim quickly through the familiar sections and take more time on the challenging parts.

Write out your plan so you don't get lost as you go. Having a written plan also helps you feel more in control of the study, so anxiety is less likely to arise from feeling overwhelmed at the amount to cover.

STEP 3: GATHER YOUR TOOLS

Decide what study method works best for you. Do you prefer to highlight in the book as you study and then go back over the highlighted portions? Or do you type out notes of the important information? Or is it helpful to make flashcards that you can carry with you? Assemble the pens, index cards, highlighters, post-it notes, and any other materials you may need so you won't be distracted by getting up to find things while you study.

If you're having a hard time retaining the information or organizing your notes, experiment with different methods. For example, try color-coding by subject with colored pens, highlighters, or post-it notes. If you learn better by hearing, try recording yourself reading your notes so you can listen while in the car, working out, or simply sitting at your desk. Ask a friend to quiz you from your flashcards, or try teaching someone the material to solidify it in your mind.

STEP 4: CREATE YOUR ENVIRONMENT

It's important to avoid distractions while you study. This includes both the obvious distractions like visitors and the subtle distractions like an uncomfortable chair (or a too-comfortable couch that makes you want to fall asleep). Set up the best study environment possible: good lighting and a comfortable work area. If background music helps you focus, you may want to turn it on, but otherwise keep the room quiet. If you are using a computer to take notes, be sure you don't have any other windows open, especially applications like social media, games, or anything else that could distract you. Silence your phone and turn off notifications. Be sure to keep water close by so you stay hydrated while you study (but avoid unhealthy drinks and snacks).

Also, take into account the best time of day to study. Are you freshest first thing in the morning? Try to set aside some time then to work through the material. Is your mind clearer in the afternoon or evening? Schedule your study session then. Another method is to study at the same time of day that you will take the test, so that your brain gets used to working on the material at that time and will be ready to focus at test time.

STEP 5: STUDY!

Once you have done all the study preparation, it's time to settle into the actual studying. Sit down, take a few moments to settle your mind so you can focus, and begin to follow your study plan. Don't give in to distractions or let yourself procrastinate. This is your time to prepare so you'll be ready to fearlessly approach the test. Make the most of the time and stay focused.

Of course, you don't want to burn out. If you study too long you may find that you're not retaining the information very well. Take regular study breaks. For example, taking five minutes out of every hour to walk briskly, breathing deeply and swinging your arms, can help your mind stay fresh.

As you get to the end of each chapter or section, it's a good idea to do a quick review. Remind yourself of what you learned and work on any difficult parts. When you feel that you've mastered the material, move on to the next part. At the end of your study session, briefly skim through your notes again.

But while review is helpful, cramming last minute is NOT. If at all possible, work ahead so that you won't need to fit all your study into the last day. Cramming overloads your brain with more information than it can process and retain, and your tired mind may struggle to recall even

How to Overcome Test Anxiety

previously learned information when it is overwhelmed with last-minute study. Also, the urgent nature of cramming and the stress placed on your brain contribute to anxiety. You'll be more likely to go to the test feeling unprepared and having trouble thinking clearly.

So don't cram, and don't stay up late before the test, even just to review your notes at a leisurely pace. Your brain needs rest more than it needs to go over the information again. In fact, plan to finish your studies by noon or early afternoon the day before the test. Give your brain the rest of the day to relax or focus on other things, and get a good night's sleep. Then you will be fresh for the test and better able to recall what you've studied.

STEP 6: TAKE A PRACTICE TEST

Many courses offer sample tests, either online or in the study materials. This is an excellent resource to check whether you have mastered the material, as well as to prepare for the test format and environment.

Check the test format ahead of time: the number of questions, the type (multiple choice, free response, etc.), and the time limit. Then create a plan for working through them. For example, if you have 30 minutes to take a 60-question test, your limit is 30 seconds per question. Spend less time on the questions you know well so that you can take more time on the difficult ones.

If you have time to take several practice tests, take the first one open book, with no time limit. Work through the questions at your own pace and make sure you fully understand them. Gradually work up to taking a test under test conditions: sit at a desk with all study materials put away and set a timer. Pace yourself to make sure you finish the test with time to spare and go back to check your answers if you have time.

After each test, check your answers. On the questions you missed, be sure you understand why you missed them. Did you misread the question (tests can use tricky wording)? Did you forget the information? Or was it something you hadn't learned? Go back and study any shaky areas that the practice tests reveal.

Taking these tests not only helps with your grade, but also aids in combating test anxiety. If you're already used to the test conditions, you're less likely to worry about it, and working through tests until you're scoring well gives you a confidence boost. Go through the practice tests until you feel comfortable, and then you can go into the test knowing that you're ready for it.

Test Tips

On test day, you should be confident, knowing that you've prepared well and are ready to answer the questions. But aside from preparation, there are several test day strategies you can employ to maximize your performance.

First, as stated before, get a good night's sleep the night before the test (and for several nights before that, if possible). Go into the test with a fresh, alert mind rather than staying up late to study.

Try not to change too much about your normal routine on the day of the test. It's important to eat a nutritious breakfast, but if you normally don't eat breakfast at all, consider eating just a protein bar. If you're a coffee drinker, go ahead and have your normal coffee. Just make sure you time it so that the caffeine doesn't wear off right in the middle of your test. Avoid sugary beverages, and drink enough water to stay hydrated but not so much that you need a restroom break 10 minutes into the test. If your test isn't first thing in the morning, consider going for a walk or doing a light workout before the test to get your blood flowing.

Allow yourself enough time to get ready, and leave for the test with plenty of time to spare so you won't have the anxiety of scrambling to arrive in time. Another reason to be early is to select a good seat. It's helpful to sit away from doors and windows, which can be distracting. Find a good seat, get out your supplies, and settle your mind before the test begins.

When the test begins, start by going over the instructions carefully, even if you already know what to expect. Make sure you avoid any careless mistakes by following the directions.

Then begin working through the questions, pacing yourself as you've practiced. If you're not sure on an answer, don't spend too much time on it, and don't let it shake your confidence. Either skip it and come back later, or eliminate as many wrong answers as possible and guess among the remaining ones. Don't dwell on these questions as you continue—put them out of your mind and focus on what lies ahead.

Be sure to read all of the answer choices, even if you're sure the first one is the right answer. Sometimes you'll find a better one if you keep reading. But don't second-guess yourself if you do immediately know the answer. Your gut instinct is usually right. Don't let test anxiety rob you of the information you know.

If you have time at the end of the test (and if the test format allows), go back and review your answers. Be cautious about changing any, since your first instinct tends to be correct, but make sure you didn't misread any of the questions or accidentally mark the wrong answer choice. Look over any you skipped and make an educated guess.

At the end, leave the test feeling confident. You've done your best, so don't waste time worrying about your performance or wishing you could change anything. Instead, celebrate the successful completion of this test. And finally, use this test to learn how to deal with anxiety even better next time.

> **Review Video: Test Anxiety**
> Visit mometrix.com/academy and enter code: 100340

Important Qualification

Not all anxiety is created equal. If your test anxiety is causing major issues in your life beyond the classroom or testing center, or if you are experiencing troubling physical symptoms related to your anxiety, it may be a sign of a serious physiological or psychological condition. If this sounds like your situation, we strongly encourage you to seek professional help.

How to Overcome Your Fear of Math

Not again. You're sitting in math class, look down at your test, and immediately start to panic. Your stomach is in knots, your heart is racing, and you break out in a cold sweat. You're staring at the paper, but everything looks like it's written in a foreign language. Even though you studied, you're blanking out on how to begin solving these problems.

Does this sound familiar? If so, then you're not alone! You may be like millions of other people who experience math anxiety. Anxiety about performing well in math is a common experience for students of all ages. In this article, we'll discuss what math anxiety is, common misconceptions about learning math, and tips and strategies for overcoming math anxiety.

What Is Math Anxiety?

Psychologist Mark H. Ashcraft explains math anxiety as a feeling of tension, apprehension, or fear that interferes with math performance. Having math anxiety negatively impacts people's beliefs about themselves and what they can achieve. It hinders achievement within the math classroom and affects the successful application of mathematics in the real world.

SYMPTOMS AND SIGNS OF MATH ANXIETY

To overcome math anxiety, you must recognize its symptoms. Becoming aware of the signs of math anxiety is the first step in addressing and resolving these fears.

NEGATIVE SELF-TALK

If you have math anxiety, you've most likely said at least one of these statements to yourself:

- "I hate math."
- "I'm not good at math."
- "I'm not a math person."

The way we speak to ourselves and think about ourselves matters. Our thoughts become our words, our words become our actions, and our actions become our habits. Thinking negatively about math creates a self-fulfilling prophecy. In other words, if you take an idea as a fact, then it will come true because your behaviors will align to match it.

AVOIDANCE

Some people who are fearful or anxious about math will tend to avoid it altogether. Avoidance can manifest in the following ways:

- Lack of engagement with math content
- Not completing homework and other assignments
- Not asking for help when needed
- Skipping class
- Avoiding math-related courses and activities

Avoidance is one of the most harmful impacts of math anxiety. If you steer clear of math at all costs, then you can't set yourself up for the success you deserve.

LACK OF MOTIVATION

Students with math anxiety may experience a lack of motivation. They may struggle to find the incentive to get engaged with what they view as a frightening subject. These students are often overwhelmed, making it difficult for them to complete or even start math assignments.

PROCRASTINATION

Another symptom of math anxiety is procrastination. Students may voluntarily delay or postpone their classwork and assignments, even if they know there will be a negative consequence for doing so. Additionally, they may choose to wait until the last minute to start projects and homework, even when they know they need more time to put forth their best effort.

PHYSIOLOGICAL REACTIONS

Many people with a fear of math experience physiological side effects. These may include an increase in heart rate, sweatiness, shakiness, nausea, and irregular breathing. These symptoms make it difficult to focus on the math content, causing the student even more stress and fear.

STRONG EMOTIONAL RESPONSES

Math anxiety also affects people on an emotional level. Responding to math content with strong emotions such as panic, anger, or despair can be a sign of math anxiety.

LOW TEST SCORES AND PERFORMANCE

Low achievement can be both a symptom and a cause of math anxiety. When someone does not take the steps needed to perform well on tests and assessments, they are less likely to pass. The more they perform poorly, the more they accept this poor performance as a fact that can't be changed.

FEELING ALONE

People who experience math anxiety feel like they are the only ones struggling, even if the math they are working on is challenging to many people. Feeling isolated in what they perceive as failure can trigger tension or nervousness.

FEELING OF PERMANENCY

Math anxiety can feel very permanent. You may assume that you are naturally bad at math and always will be. Viewing math as a natural ability rather than a skill that can be learned causes people to believe that nothing will help them improve. They take their current math abilities as fact and assume that they can't be changed. As a result, they give up, stop trying to improve, and avoid engaging with math altogether.

LACK OF CONFIDENCE

People with low self-confidence in math tend to feel awkward and incompetent when asked to solve a math problem. They don't feel comfortable taking chances or risks when problem-solving because they second-guess themselves and assume they are incorrect. They don't trust in their ability to learn the content and solve problems correctly.

PANIC

A general sense of unexplained panic is also a sign of math anxiety. You may feel a sudden sense of fear that triggers physical reactions, even when there is no apparent reason for such a response.

How to Overcome Your Fear of Math

127

Causes of Math Anxiety

Math anxiety can start at a young age and may have one or more underlying causes. Common causes of math anxiety include the following:

The Attitude of Parents or Guardians

Parents often put pressure on their children to perform well in school. Although their intentions are usually good, this pressure can lead to anxiety, especially if the student is struggling with a subject or class.

Perhaps your parents or others in your life hold negative predispositions about math based on their own experiences. For instance, if your mother once claimed she was not good at math, then you might have incorrectly interpreted this as a predisposed trait that was passed down to you.

Teacher Influence

Students often pick up on their teachers' attitudes about the content being taught. If a teacher is happy and excited about math, students are more likely to mirror these emotions. However, if a teacher lacks enthusiasm or genuine interest, then students are more inclined to disengage.

Teachers have a responsibility to cultivate a welcoming classroom culture that is accepting of mistakes. When teachers blame students for not understanding a concept, they create a hostile classroom environment where mistakes are not tolerated. This tension increases student stress and anxiety, creating conditions that are not conducive to inquiry and learning. Instead, when teachers normalize mistakes as a natural part of the problem-solving process, they give their students the freedom to explore and grapple with the math content. In such an environment, students feel comfortable taking chances because they are not afraid of being wrong.

Students need teachers that can help when they're having problems understanding difficult concepts. In doing so, educators may need to change how they teach the content. Since different people have unique learning styles, it's the job of the teacher to adapt to the needs of each student. Additionally, teachers should encourage students to explore alternate problem-solving strategies, even if it's not the preferred method of the educator.

Fear of Being Wrong

Embarrassing situations can be traumatic, especially for young children and adolescents. These experiences can stay with people through their adult lives. Those with math anxiety may experience a fear of being wrong, especially in front of a group of peers. This fear can be paralyzing, interfering with the student's concentration and ability to focus on the problem at hand.

Timed Assessments

Timed assessments can help improve math fluency, but they often create unnecessary pressure for students to complete an unrealistic number of problems within a specified timeframe. Many studies have shown that timed assessments often result in increased levels of anxiety, reducing a student's overall competence and ability to problem-solve.

128

Debunking Math Myths

There are lots of myths about math that are related to the causes and development of math-related anxiety. Although these myths have been proven to be false, many people take them as fact. Let's go over a few of the most common myths about learning math.

MYTH: MEN ARE BETTER AT MATH THAN WOMEN

Math has a reputation for being a male-dominant subject, but this doesn't mean that men are inherently better at math than women. Many famous mathematical discoveries have been made by women. Katherine Johnson, Dame Mary Lucy Cartwright, and Marjorie Lee Brown are just a few of the many famous women mathematicians. Expecting to be good or bad at math because of your gender sets you up for stress and confusion. Math is a skill that can be learned, just like cooking or riding a bike.

MYTH: THERE IS ONLY ONE GOOD WAY TO SOLVE MATH PROBLEMS

There are many ways to get the correct answer when it comes to math. No two people have the same brain, so everyone takes a slightly different approach to problem-solving. Moreover, there isn't one way of problem-solving that's superior to another. Your way of working through a problem might differ from someone else's, and that is okay. Math can be a highly individualized process, so the best method for you should be the one that makes you feel the most comfortable and makes the most sense to you.

MYTH: MATH REQUIRES A GOOD MEMORY

For many years, mathematics was taught through memorization. However, learning in such a way hinders the development of critical thinking and conceptual understanding. These skill sets are much more valuable than basic memorization. For instance, you might be great at memorizing mathematical formulas, but if you don't understand what they mean, then you can't apply them to different scenarios in the real world. When a student is working from memory, they are limited in the strategies available to them to problem-solve. In other words, they assume there is only one correct way to do the math, which is the method they memorized. Having a variety of problem-solving options can help students figure out which method works best for them. Additionally, it provides students with a better understanding of how and why certain mathematical strategies work. While memorization can be helpful in some instances, it is not an absolute requirement for mathematicians.

MYTH: MATH IS NOT CREATIVE

Math requires imagination and intuition. Contrary to popular belief, it is a highly creative field. Mathematical creativity can help in developing new ways to think about and solve problems. Many people incorrectly assume that all things are either creative or analytical. However, this black-and-white view is limiting because the field of mathematics involves both creativity and logic.

MYTH: MATH ISN'T SUPPOSED TO BE FUN

Whoever told you that math isn't supposed to be fun is a liar. There are tons of math-based activities and games that foster friendly competition and engagement. Math is often best learned through play, and lots of mobile apps and computer games exemplify this.

Additionally, math can be an exceptionally collaborative and social experience. Studying or working through problems with a friend often makes the process a lot more fun. The excitement and satisfaction of solving a difficult problem with others is quite rewarding. Math can be fun if you look for ways to make it more collaborative and enjoyable.

MYTH: NOT EVERYONE IS CAPABLE OF LEARNING MATH

There's no such thing as a "math person." Although many people think that you're either good at math or you're not, this is simply not true. Everyone is capable of learning and applying mathematics. However, not everyone learns the same way. Since each person has a different learning style, the trick is to find the strategies and learning tools that work best for you. Some people learn best through hands-on experiences, and others find success through the use of visual aids. Others are auditory learners and learn best by hearing and listening. When people are overwhelmed or feel that math is too hard, it's often because they haven't found the learning strategy that works best for them.

MYTH: GOOD MATHEMATICIANS WORK QUICKLY AND NEVER MAKE MISTAKES

There is no prize for finishing first in math. It's not a race, and speed isn't a measure of your ability. Good mathematicians take their time to ensure their work is accurate. As you gain more experience and practice, you will naturally become faster and more confident.

Additionally, everyone makes mistakes, including good mathematicians. Mistakes are a normal part of the problem-solving process, and they're not a bad thing. The important thing is that we take the time to learn from our mistakes, understand where our misconceptions are, and move forward.

MYTH: YOU DON'T NEED MATH IN THE REAL WORLD

Our day-to-day lives are so infused with mathematical concepts that we often don't even realize when we're using math in the real world. In fact, most people tend to underestimate how much we do math in our everyday lives. It's involved in an enormous variety of daily activities such as shopping, baking, finances, and gardening, as well as in many careers, including architecture, nursing, design, and sales.

Tips and Strategies for Overcoming Math Anxiety

If your anxiety is getting in the way of your level of mathematical engagement, then there are lots of steps you can take. Check out the strategies below to start building confidence in math today.

FOCUS ON UNDERSTANDING, NOT MEMORIZATION

Don't drive yourself crazy trying to memorize every single formula or mathematical process. Instead, shift your attention to understanding concepts. Those who prioritize memorization over conceptual understanding tend to have lower achievement levels in math. Students who memorize may be able to complete some math, but they don't understand the process well enough to apply it to different situations. Memorization comes with time and practice, but it won't help alleviate math anxiety. On the other hand, conceptual understanding will give you the building blocks of knowledge you need to build up your confidence.

REPLACE NEGATIVE SELF-TALK WITH POSITIVE SELF-TALK

Start to notice how you think about yourself. Whenever you catch yourself thinking something negative, try replacing that thought with a positive affirmation. Instead of continuing the negative thought, pause to reframe the situation. For ideas on how to get started, take a look at the table below:

Instead of thinking...	Try thinking...
"I can't do this math." "I'm not a math person."	"I'm up for the challenge, and I'm training my brain in math."
"This problem is too hard."	"This problem is hard, so this might take some time and effort. I know I can do this."
"I give up."	"What strategies can help me solve this problem?"
"I made a mistake, so I'm not good at this."	"Everyone makes mistakes. Mistakes help me to grow and understand."
"I'll never be smart enough."	"I can figure this out, and I am smart enough."

PRACTICE MINDFULNESS

Practicing mindfulness and focusing on your breathing can help alleviate some of the physical symptoms of math anxiety. By taking deep breaths, you can remind your nervous system that you are not in immediate danger. Doing so will reduce your heart rate and help with any irregular breathing or shakiness. Taking the edge off of the physiological effects of anxiety will clear your mind, allowing your brain to focus its energy on problem-solving.

DO SOME MATH EVERY DAY

Think about learning math as if you were learning a foreign language. If you don't use it, you lose it. If you don't practice your math skills regularly, you'll have a harder time achieving comprehension and fluency. Set some amount of time aside each day, even if it's just for a few minutes, to practice. It might take some discipline to build a habit around this, but doing so will help increase your mathematical self-assurance.

USE ALL OF YOUR RESOURCES

Everyone has a different learning style, and there are plenty of resources out there to support all learners. When you get stuck on a math problem, think about the tools you have access to, and use them when applicable. Such resources may include flashcards, graphic organizers, study guides, interactive notebooks, and peer study groups. All of these are great tools to accommodate your individual learning style. Finding the tools and resources that work for your learning style will give you the confidence you need to succeed.

REALIZE THAT YOU AREN'T ALONE

Remind yourself that lots of other people struggle with math anxiety, including teachers, nurses, and even successful mathematicians. You aren't the only one who panics when faced with a new or challenging problem. It's probably much more common than you think. Realizing that you aren't alone in your experience can help put some distance between yourself and the emotions you feel about math. It also helps to normalize the anxiety and shift your perspective.

How to Overcome Your Fear of Math

131

ASK QUESTIONS

If there's a concept you don't understand and you've tried everything you can, then it's okay to ask for help! You can always ask your teacher or professor for help. If you're not learning math in a traditional classroom, you may want to join a study group, work with a tutor, or talk to your friends. More often than not, you aren't the only one of your peers who needs clarity on a mathematical concept. Seeking understanding is a great way to increase self-confidence in math.

REMEMBER THAT THERE'S MORE THAN ONE WAY TO SOLVE A PROBLEM

Since everyone learns differently, it's best to focus on understanding a math problem with an approach that makes sense to you. If the way it's being taught is confusing to you, don't give up. Instead, work to understand the problem using a different technique. There's almost always more than one problem-solving method when it comes to math. Don't get stressed if one of them doesn't make sense to you. Instead, shift your focus to what does make sense. Chances are high that you know more than you think you do.

VISUALIZATION

Visualization is the process of creating images in your mind's eye. Picture yourself as a successful, confident mathematician. Think about how you would feel and how you would behave. What would your work area look like? How would you organize your belongings? The more you focus on something, the more likely you are to achieve it. Visualizing teaches your brain that you can achieve whatever it is that you want. Thinking about success in mathematics will lead to acting like a successful mathematician. This, in turn, leads to actual success.

FOCUS ON THE EASIEST PROBLEMS FIRST

To increase your confidence when working on a math test or assignment, try solving the easiest problems first. Doing so will remind you that you are successful in math and that you do have what it takes. This process will increase your belief in yourself, giving you the confidence you need to tackle more complex problems.

FIND A SUPPORT GROUP

A study buddy, tutor, or peer group can go a long way in decreasing math-related anxiety. Such support systems offer lots of benefits, including a safe place to ask questions, additional practice with mathematical concepts, and an understanding of other problem-solving explanations that may work better for you. Equipping yourself with a support group is one of the fastest ways to eliminate math anxiety.

REWARD YOURSELF FOR WORKING HARD

Recognize the amount of effort you're putting in to overcome your math anxiety. It's not an easy task, so you deserve acknowledgement. Surround yourself with people who will provide you with the positive reinforcement you deserve.

Remember, You Can Do This!

Conquering a fear of math can be challenging, but there are lots of strategies that can help you out. Your own beliefs about your mathematical capabilities can limit your potential. Working toward a growth mindset can have a tremendous impact on decreasing math-related anxiety and building confidence. By knowing the symptoms of math anxiety and recognizing common misconceptions about learning math, you can develop a plan to address your fear of math. Utilizing the strategies discussed can help you overcome this anxiety and build the confidence you need to succeed.

Tell Us Your Story

We at Mometrix would like to extend our heartfelt thanks to you for letting us be a part of your journey. It is an honor to serve people from all walks of life, people like you, who are committed to building the best future they can for themselves.

We know that each person's situation is unique. But we also know that, whether you are a young student or a mother of four, you care about working to make your own life and the lives of those around you better.

That's why we want to hear your story.

We want to know why you're taking this test. We want to know about the trials you've gone through to get here. And we want to know about the successes you've experienced after taking and passing your test.

In addition to your story, which can be an inspiration both to us and to others, we value your feedback. We want to know both what you loved about our book and what you think we can improve on.

The team at Mometrix would be absolutely thrilled to hear from you! So please, send us an email at tellusyourstory@mometrix.com or visit us at mometrix.com/tellusyourstory.php and let's stay in touch.

Additional Bonus Material

Due to our efforts to try to keep this book to a manageable length, we've created a link that will give you access to all of your additional bonus material:

mometrix.com/bonus948/gmat

Made in the USA
Middletown, DE
18 June 2025

77196334R00080